The

Gospel

in

Miniature

. . .

Meditations for When
You Have a Minute

MARTIN B. COPENHAVER

Walking Together, Finding the Way®

SKYLIGHT PATHS®
PUBLISHING
Nashville, Tennessee

SkyLight Paths Publishing
an imprint of Turner Publishing Company
Nashville, Tennessee
New York, New York
www.skylightpaths.com
www.turnerpublishing.com

The Gospel in Miniature: Meditations for When You Have a Minute

For information regarding permission to reprint material from this book, please write or fax your request to Turner Publishing, Permissions Department, at 4507 Charlotte Avenue, Suite 100, Nashville, Tennessee, 37209, (615) 255-2665, fax (615) 255-5081, or email your request to submissions@turnerpublishing.com.

Unless otherwise indicated, scripture quotations are taken from the *New Revised Standard Version*, copyright © 1989, 1995 by the Division of Christian Education of the National Council of the Churches of Christ in the United States of America. Used by permission. All rights reserved.

Library of Congress Cataloging-in-Publication Data upon request

18 19 20 21 • 10 9 8 7 6 5 4 3 2 1

Manufactured in the United States of America
Cover Design: Maddie Cothren
Interior Design: Tim Holtz

I have always been told that my brother, Chad, and my sister, Jan, jumped up and down on their beds in exuberant celebration when our father announced my birth. That is not hard for me to imagine, because I have felt their love and care for me throughout my entire life. It is with great gratitude that I dedicate this book to them.

Introduction

This book borrows its title from Martin Luther, who described a single verse of the Bible (John 3:16) as "the gospel in miniature." I have always loved Luther's phrase because it underscores what Jesus consistently points our attention to: the way God can be seen at work in small things like mustard seeds, pinches of yeast, the tiniest of coins, and the smallest of children. And, of course, Jesus taught through parables, one of the shortest of all literary forms. It is fitting that the parable of the mustard seed, in praise of smallness, is itself small—only two verses long (Luke 13:18–19).

The devotions in this book originally appeared as *Stillspeaking* daily devotionals, emailed each day to subscribers by my denomination, the United Church of Christ. The name comes from our tradition's affirmation that God communicated to people not only long ago, but also now, if we are attentive. Revelation is unfolding and continues to unfold. "God is still speaking" is the way we have summarized that understanding.

From the beginning, those of us who were writing devotions believed they had to be short enough to fit on a computer screen. So we were limited to 250 words. That presented something of a challenge to the writers, who were mostly preachers for whom 250 words felt like clearing your throat before getting started. It can be challenging to write something so brief. As Mark Twain once wrote to a friend, "Sorry I wrote you such a long post; I didn't have time for a shorter one."

Over time, however, I learned that writing in such a form was a helpful discipline. I had to get right to the point, and it could be only one point, no more. Words were too precious to waste. Writing such short pieces also became a way to affirm—and experience—that our understanding of the gospel seldom comes on a grand scale; rather, more often our understanding comes in glimpses and momentary flashes of insight.

This book is not like others where you have to begin at the beginning and proceed dutifully through each successive page until you reach the end. You can read this book in that orderly way, but you don't have to. I remember hearing that novelist James Joyce contended that a good novel should be able to have its pages thrown to the four winds, picked up in random order, and read in that sequence without losing any of the novel's meaning. I have never been able to picture that being true for a novel, but I know it is true of this book. You can start wherever you like, perhaps hovering over the individual entries as you would over a box of chocolates, until you find one you think you will enjoy.

My hope is that some of my glimpses of the gospel, as recorded in this book, will become occasions for your own glimpses as well.

A Messy Desk

All have sinned and fall short of the glory of God.
—from Romans 3:21–26 NIV

I have always had a messy desk. I used to claim that it was actually more efficient not to spend all that time filing things away. I even seemed to take pride in surveying the mountain ranges of papers on my desk and somehow being able to pull out just the right one. I dubbed my desk a "wilderness of free association."

Every once in a while, I would put everything away, which was never a permanent solution, but more like pruning to allow for further growth.

But, to be honest, I felt self-conscious about my messy desk. All my colleagues have tidy desks. If their desks were beds, they would have hospital corners.

Then one day a parishioner came into my office, looked at my messy desk, and said, "Martin, you've got to get it together. If you can't hold it together, what hope is there for the rest of us?"

Ever since she said that, I have made a point of not cleaning my desk. The mess is a reminder to me, and to anyone who comes into my office, that I don't have it together and that, indeed, none of us does. And a messy desk is the least of it. Our lives, in various ways and to varying degrees, are not tidy or properly ordered. "All have sinned and fall short of the glory of God" is the way Paul put it.

So I no longer claim that my messy desk is more efficient. I don't call it a wilderness of free association. Now I think of it as a call to confession.

Prayer
God, let's look together at the mess and if, for whatever reason, I cannot clean it up, hear my prayer of confession. Amen.

Who's That Knocking at My Door?

*Listen! I am standing at the door, knocking; if you
hear my voice and open the door, I will come in
to you and eat with you, and you with me.*

—from Revelation 3:15–22

In the Rule of Benedict, the remarkable document that has ordered the life of Benedictine monks for fifteen hundred years, there is a particular role delineated for the "porter" of the monastery. Quite simply, the porter is the one who opens the door to the monastery when someone knocks. Not much of a role, you say? Ah, but there is so much to it. Author Joan Chittister goes so far as to say, "The way we answer doors is the way we deal with the world."

So the porter is given very specific instructions. As soon as anyone knocks, likely a poor person—because they often sought refuge in monasteries—the porter is to reply, "Thanks be to God." That's before he even knows who is on the other side of the door. Isn't that remarkable?

The author Dorothy Parker, famous for her dark wit, used to answer her telephone with this greeting: "What fresh hell is this?"

What do you think when someone knocks on your door? Is it closer to "What fresh hell is this?" or to "Thanks be to God"?

And why is the porter in a Benedictine monastery so quick to respond when someone knocks on the door? It is not just out of some general sense that it is the right thing to do. Rather, the porter immediately gets up to respond because it might be Jesus knocking on the door. Not Jesus as we have ever encountered him before, but Jesus just the same. As an old Celtic saying has it, "Oft, oft, oft goes Christ in stranger's guise."

So when a porter—or someone of a porter's spirit—hears a knock on the door, he doesn't delay in showing hospitality. No, instead, he gets up and declares, "Thanks be to God," because it could be Jesus. And often—oft, oft, oft—it is.

Prayer

Jesus, help me to welcome a stranger in the manner I would welcome you. Amen.

Excuses, Excuses, Excuses

Jesus said to him, "Someone gave a great dinner and
invited many. . . . But they all alike began to make excuses."
—from Luke 14:15–24

Early in our marriage, my wife, Karen, and I got tickets to see
The Elephant Man, which at the time was the hottest show on
Broadway.

At dinner before the show, I took the tickets out of my pocket.
(I'm with Charlie Brown, who said, "Happiness is holding the
tickets in your hand.") But as I looked at the tickets, my face
went ashen. They were good seats all right, but the tickets were for
Tuesday night and this was Wednesday. We were a day late.

We quickly paid the bill and headed over to the theater. I
showed the tickets to the ticket taker at the door and told him
the story of how we ended up with tickets for the wrong night.
Before I could get very far, however, he pointed to a corner of
the lobby and said, "Wait over there for Miss Morris."

We waited anxiously to speak to Miss Morris, although
we were sure we had a unique tale of woe. After a few min-
utes passed, I saw the ticket taker talking to others and then
pointing to the corner where we were standing. Tentatively, we
began to share our stories. One couple left their tickets at home.
A woman said she picked up the wrong purse when she left
her house. Two folks had an excuse very similar to mine—they
had not noticed that their tickets were for the matinee performance that day and not the evening performance. Everyone had
their excuses. In one another's company, however, our excuses
no longer seemed compelling or unique. They became rather
embarrassing.

Eventually, Miss Morris came over to our little group,
patiently listened to our stories, and let us into the theater—for
standing room.

I wonder how many excuses the omnipotent Miss Morris hears every day. And if Miss Morris hears a lot of excuses, I wonder how many excuses God hears every day.

Prayer

God, please take my excuses and exchange them for confessions and a reliance upon your grace. Amen.

Jesus's Lost and Found Collection

Which one of you, having a hundred sheep and losing one
of them, does not leave the ninety-nine in the wilderness
and go after the one that is lost until he finds it?

—from Luke 15:3–7

One of the legendary professors at my seminary was Roland Bainton, a historian and the author of many books. When I knew him, he was in his eighties, and he still wrote a book every other year. He would quip, "When you have reached my age, the expression 'publish or perish' takes on new meaning."

Every day he would ride his bicycle between the library and his home. During the winter, he wore a thin overcoat and gloves, but the gloves never matched. He might, for instance, wear one ski mitten and one oversized leather glove. I once heard him explain, "I found them all riding my bicycle up Prospect Street—I suppose I go slowly enough to spot them—and I just put them to use." And somehow, on the hands of this great man, the gloves—as different as they were—seemed to go together, as if they were part of a set.

This memory has become something of parable for me, reminding me of the parable that is our scripture for today. There is one who carefully treks the byways, pausing to pick up those people who have been cast off or lost, then he puts them to use. And somehow, in his caring hands, those he picks up do not seem motley or mismatched. Rather, as different as we are, we go together, as if we are part of a set. Once cast off and alone, now we are gathered up in love and brought together for service.

Prayer

O God of the last, the least, and the lost, I am grateful that you do not wait for me to come to you, but that you seek me out and gather me in. Amen.

Terrible Taste in Friends

When the Pharisees saw this, they said to
his disciples, "Why does your teacher eat
with tax collectors and sinners?"
—from Matthew 9:10–12

I have a friend who has terrible taste in friends. So, I must confess, I usually greet invitations to dinner parties at her home with a bit of dread. I fear that I will not like the company I will be asked to keep at her table. Will I once again be asked to sit next to someone whose extreme political views I find hard to stomach? If that conservative Christian is there this time, will he feel as if he has to set me straight yet again?

I wish this friend of mine were more discriminating. If she could just have better taste in friends . . .

Then, eventually, I remind myself that *I* am her friend and that I may benefit from her terrible taste in friends as well. The door to her heart is wide enough to accommodate a most motley bunch. Including me, apparently.

In one particularly pernicious church fight, two contending parties really went at it. It got ugly. Divisions widened. Finally, someone stood up and said, "I figure if I can put up with the two of you, you ought to be able to put up with each other."

Sometimes it seems as if Jesus has terrible taste in friends. And, of course, I am among them. But, in essence, Jesus says to the church, "If I can put up with all of you, you ought to be able to put up with one another."

Prayer
Jesus, I am grateful that you eat with sinners, because then I know there is room at the table for me. Amen.

But Can You Dance to It?

They are like children sitting in the marketplace
and calling to one another, "We played the
flute for you, and you did not dance."
—from Luke 7:24–35

Among the most noncommittal people in the world are young teenagers at their first dance. They stand at the edge of the dance floor, all hands and no place to put them. They assume a look that struggles to be casual. The look says, "Don't think I came here on purpose. Somehow I just ended up in this place."

Looking in on this scene you might wonder, "What are they waiting for, anyway? Waiting for the right dance partner to look in their direction? Waiting for the right song? Waiting to be a few years older?"

Jesus said people can be very much like that when it comes to religious commitment—they refuse to dance. They are like those who sit in chairs around the edge of the hall for the entire evening. They listen through waltz after foxtrot after tango after jitterbug without so much as tapping a toe. Finally, the piano player decides he's had enough: "Hey, what do you folks want, anyway?"

"We'll know it when we hear it," they reply. "Nothing you've played so far."

Some people avoid religious commitment in a similar way. Nothing is ever quite right. Their song is never played, or so it seems.

Those who remain forever on the sidelines may avoid the risk of commitment, but they will never experience the joy of dancing. And the music always sounds better on the dance floor than it does from the sidelines.

As author Gertrude Stein once observed, "You look ridiculous if you dance. You look ridiculous if you don't dance. So you might as well dance."

Prayer

God, don't let me remain forever noncommittal. Get me on the dance floor so that I can truly hear the music. Amen.

Memory and Personhood

Can a woman forget her nursing child, or show
no compassion for the child of her womb? Even
these may forget, yet I will not forget you. See, I
have inscribed you on the palms of my hands.
—from Isaiah 49:14–18

When my father died, we went to tell my grandmother the news, news she was not able to comprehend. In a sense, dementia saved her from grief, so there was some comfort in that. Yet still, her only child had died and it seemed unspeakably sad that she could not recognize his name or mark the loss. The prophet Isaiah asked, "Can a woman forget her child?" In the case of my grandmother, the answer would have to be yes.

When my grandmother herself died a number of years later, we said things like, "She left us a long time ago."

Our memories are so much a part of who we are that it can be hard to imagine who we would be without them. In some sense, we are what we remember.

But, just as surely, we are more than our memories. We do not say of an infant, in those early months before memory, "Well, she's not yet arrived. She's not yet a person."

A loss of memory does not make us any less a person. And those who no longer can remember the prayers of the church, or the Bible stories, or the hymns, have a special place in the church. The church is a community that remembers the prayers and stories for you and sings the hymns on your behalf when you no longer can.

In the end, what ensures our personhood is that we are remembered by God.

Isaiah asks, "Can a woman forget her nursing child, or show no compassion for the child of her womb?" And the answer is, "Yes. Tragically, sometimes yes." But Isaiah quickly adds these words, which he takes to be God's very assurance: "Even these may forget, yet I will not forget you. See, I have inscribed you on the palms of my hands."

Prayer

God, remember me, even when others forget, or when I may forget your promises. Inscribe me on the palms of your hands. Amen.

Look Who's Watching

Put these things into practice, devote yourselves
to them, so that all may see your progress. Pay
close attention to yourself and your teaching;
continue in these things, for in doing this you
will save both yourself and your hearers.

—from 1 Timothy 4:6–16

I was once asked to recruit some folks to stand outside the entrance of our local supermarket on a December Saturday to solicit contributions for the Salvation Army. All the volunteers were asked to do is stand beside a red bucket and ring a bell. I thought I should take a turn myself. It was fascinating to see how people responded.

I noticed that there were two groups who responded in extraordinary numbers: First, there were the members of my church. I like to think that they would have responded that way no matter who was ringing the bell, but all I can say for sure is that every church member who passed me put a contribution in the bucket.

The others who responded with particular generosity were adults with children at their side. And the reason seems clear enough: They knew that there were very important eyes on them—the eyes of their children. Knowing that they were being observed by their children helped them draw on the better angels of their nature. They became more generous than they would have been otherwise.

That experience also was an important reminder to me, to parents and grandparents, and to all who have some special tie to a child: There is nothing we can give our children—no toy, no trip, no tuition—that is more important than the gift of our generosity to others. It is the one thing that will not and cannot be taken away from them.

Prayer

God, help me to seize an opportunity to be more generous today, as if young eyes were trained on me because ... well, they are. Amen.

Awaiting Further Light

Without any doubt, the mystery of our religion is great.
—from 1 Timothy 3:14–16

We all have files in our minds labeled Accepted and Rejected. As we hear or read something, we usually feel obliged to put it in one file or the other. Those who seek to grow in their faith, however, also have an additional file labeled Awaiting Further Light.

Obviously, such a file will not be found in the mind of the fanatic (the person who could be described as believing what God would believe if God had all the facts). Those who make liberal use of the file labeled Awaiting Further Light exhibit a humility that is not found in the fanatic believer or disbeliever.

Having an active Awaiting Further Light file demonstrates openness to new truth and unfolding experience. Such a file will be filled with all those things that do not yet clearly belong in either the Accepted file or the Rejected file. For those who seek to grow in their faith, such a file may also include many traditional Christian beliefs that we might be inclined to put in the Rejected file were it not for the voices of historic Christian witnesses who counsel, "Not so fast. You may not fully believe this now, but please trust us enough to put it somewhere where you will be sure to consider it again."

Rainer Maria Rilke once gave this famous advice to a young poet: "I want to beg you to be patient toward all that is unsolved in your heart and try to love the questions themselves." That's good advice because, as the author of 1 Timothy observed, "The mystery of our religion is great."

Prayer
O mysterious God, please give me patience toward all that is unresolved in my heart. Amen.

To Save or to Savor?

Mary took a pound of costly perfume
made of pure nard, anointed Jesus' feet,
and wiped them with her hair.

—from John 12:1–11

E. B. White once observed, "If the world were merely seductive, that would be easy. If it were merely challenging, that would be no problem. But I arise in the morning torn between a desire to improve the world and a desire to enjoy the world. That makes it hard to plan the day."

In planning our days, confused as we are about how to spend them, we may wonder if the answer is found in moderation. But Jesus refused to criticize the woman who anointed him with lavish amounts of costly perfume. It seems that Jesus thinks we are meant to get carried away from time to time.

The Christian life is not so much about moderation. Instead, it is about rhythm. There is, indeed, a time to serve the world and a time to savor the world. To be sure, one can get stuck on one side of this dynamic, which can be about as dangerous as only inhaling or only exhaling. The dangers of only savoring the world are clear: this leads to a life of self-indulgence. But, just as certainly, there are dangers in only serving the world. To only serve and never to savor the world is to be only the giver of gifts and never the receiver. It means that we never have to admit our need or to say thank you.

So we are called to do both—to serve and to savor—not at the same time, perhaps, because that may not be possible, but each in turn at the appropriate time. Which is another way of saying that our life depends on being inconsistent in the way all who both breathe in and breathe out are inconsistent.

Prayer

O God, help me both to serve and to savor—and to know which I am called to do at this time. Amen.

Feeling Small

The heavens are telling the glory of God.
—from Psalm 19

A friend once teased me that my idea of a picnic is to go to a French restaurant and open the windows. And it is true that, for the most part, I am a lover of the great indoors. That is where I most often encounter God: in human community, through art and books, and through one book in particular. So when I hear "The heavens are telling the glory of God," I do not immediately picture a star-bejeweled night. Rather, I hear Haydn's wonderful musical setting of that psalm.

But there are times when I have been overcome with awe at God's creation. For instance, when I stand at the lapping fringe of the ocean, gazing at the seemingly limitless horizon, it serves as a living reminder to me of the greatness and power of God.

I have heard that when Theodore Roosevelt was president, he used to entertain naturalist William Beebe at his home at Sagamore Hill. After the evening's conversation, the two would go out on the lawn and gaze up at the sky. Then one or the other would ritually recite, "That is the spiral galaxy of Andromeda. It is as large as our Milky Way. It has a hundred million suns, each larger than our own." After an interval, Roosevelt would grin at Beebe and say, "Now I think we're small enough. We can go to bed."

Every once in a while, it is good to be reminded of just how small we are. But there is a second reminder that is just as important: God loves small things, perhaps most of all.

Prayer
God, today I thank you for the way your creation bears witness to your greatness; and yet you care for each of your creatures, including me. Amen.

Belief and Faith Are Different

The Lord is my strength and my
shield; in him my heart trusts.
—from Psalm 28

People sometimes use the words *belief* and *faith* as if they were synonyms. They do have much in common, but they are different as well.

Imagine that you are at a circus. A skilled high-wire artist has accomplished many marvelous feats that inspire awe in the audience. Then the ringmaster addresses the crowd: "Ladies and gentlemen, if you believe that this daring man can ride safely over the high wire on his bicycle while carrying someone on his shoulders, please raise your hand." Seeing an almost unanimous vote of confidence, the ringmaster says, "Very well, then. Now who would like to be the first to volunteer to sit on his shoulders?"

The difference between belief and faith is the difference between raising your hand and getting on the high-wire artist's shoulders. Faith is not passive or merely intellectual. To believe in God, all you need say is "This is true," but to have faith in God, you must go on to say "Yes, I will."

Belief, in itself, is not enough. We may believe that God has "the whole world in his hands," but faith is the act of trust by which we put ourselves into God's hands. The real synonym for *faith* is *trust*. You can sit back and believe, but faith requires you to get out of your seat. Faith is the active expression of trust.

Prayer
O God, whatever I might believe or not believe about you, help me to entrust myself to your care at every turn and in every hour this day. Amen.

Interruptions

And Mary said, "My soul
magnifies the Lord, and my spirit
rejoices in God my Savior."

—from Luke 1:46–55

For the most part, I don't like interruptions. I would rather plan my day and plan my life. So usually I begin the day by surveying all the things I want to accomplish and hope no interruption will keep me from doing so.

I say that as a confession, because interruptions are one of God's preferred modes of confronting us. The word *interruption* means, literally, "something that breaks in between." We may experience interruptions as our routine breaking up, but it may be that God is trying to *break in* to our lives.

It is remarkable how the characters in the Bible respond to having their lives interrupted. For instance, Mary's plans to marry are interrupted by an angel who tells her that she is about give birth to the Son of the Most High, even though she is hardly more than a child herself. How does she respond to this interruption of her plans? She sings a song of praise.

The very birth the angel proclaims is itself an interruption. It is God interrupting God's own routine by coming as a little one, born in a forgotten corner of a big world. And when God chooses to come as close to human life as breath and bone and muscle, we can't look at our own lives in the same way again.

It's not a story we would have come up with ourselves. It's nothing we would have planned. In a way, it's an interruption. But in hearing this story again, perhaps we have a chance to put our plans aside long enough to greet an interruption as welcome. After all, it could be God breaking in.

Prayer

God, don't listen to me when I ask not to be interrupted. Break in. Break in. Amen.

My Brother, the Cowboy

In our own languages we hear them
speaking about God's deeds of power.
—from Acts 2:1–13

A while back I heard a story on the radio about a "cowboy church" in Fort Worth, Texas. It meets in the bull-riding ring of a huge bar called Billy Bob's. On Saturday night, cowboys lean against the bar. On Sunday morning, some of these same people are back in the same arena, the smell of stale beer clinging to the sawdust scattered on the floor, to hear a former champion calf roper preach the gospel under signs that advertise SKOAL chewing tobacco and LONE STAR beer. The minister's name is Jeff Copenhaver.

I had never heard of this fellow before. The news that I might have a calf-ropin', gospel-preachin' cousin in Texas was almost too much to grasp.

The radio excerpts from Copenhaver's sermons: "As a cowboy, you learn that you gotta keep your hat low on your head so that it won't fall off. It's the same with the gospel of Jesus Christ."

The voice on the radio kept referring to him as "Mr. Copenhaver." Couldn't they have specified, "The other Mr. Copenhaver, the one in Texas, who preaches in a bull-riding arena using homely images drawn from his life as a cowboy, said . . ."?

I often recall this story on Pentecost because that was the day when the diverse followers of Jesus were drawn together by the Holy Spirit. They were unified in a way that only the Spirit can achieve.

So, in the spirit of Pentecost, I will claim you as part of my family, Jeff Copenhaver, and the next time I am in Fort Worth, I will worship with you. You may not be a cousin, but you are a brother.

Prayer

Come, Holy Spirit, come! Take our motley gatherings and make us one body—the church. Amen.

Marty

Rejoice always, pray continually.
—1 Thessalonians 5:16–17 NIV

In the Academy Award–winning movie *Marty*, Ernest Borgnine plays the title character, a homely butcher who lives in Brooklyn. Marty is in his late thirties and lives with his mother. He spends Saturday nights hanging around with his friend Angie.

Marty is not comfortable around women because, in his own words, he is just "a fat, ugly man." So he usually clams up around women.

One night, Marty goes with Angie to the Stardust Ballroom, and he is offered five dollars by a stranger to escort home the man's unattractive blind date. Angie assumes Marty will turn down the offer, describing the woman as "a real dog." But, instead, Marty turns down the money and approaches the woman. The two dance a bit, then Marty walks her to the bus stop.

When they reach the bus stop, Marty and the woman keep on going because they are lost in conversation. The woman listens attentively and with appreciation. Sensing this, Marty speaks from the heart in a flood of words. He talks about his work, his family, his worries, his hopes—thoughts he has never expressed and some he has expressed but which have never been fully heard.

Occasionally, Marty interrupts himself: "Gee, I just can't stop talkin'. I'm going to let you talk now." Then the woman says something that triggers a new thought for Marty, and he is talking again. The woman smiles until Marty stops himself again: "Gee, there I go again! I just can't stop talkin'. What is this?"

What is this, Marty? It is the easy flow of conversation with someone who accepts you just as you are.

And that is what prayer is.

Prayer

God, because you accept me just as I am, I know you accept my prayers just as they are. Amen.

Consider the Lilies, If You Can

Consider the lilies of the field, how they
grow; they neither toil nor spin, yet I
tell you, even Solomon in all his glory
was not clothed like one of these.

—from Matthew 6:25–34

Summer is the time when I can cross items off my to-do list. Not that I have completed them. I just cross them off.

I have a tendency to approach the summer as if it were the repository of all that I have not accomplished during the year. I imagine that in the summer I will have time to clean my closets, organize my files, write those articles that are soon due, and so much more. In this scenario, summer is the time to catch up.

But somewhere near the end of July, I begin to cross items off my to-do list. Most of them aren't going to get done this summer—again. It happens almost every year—summer starts out being about work and ends up being about grace.

To be sure, we still have work to do in the summer, but summer was made for more than work. It is a time to let the tempo of the year slow down to an adagio. It is a time for relishing God's creation and the company of others. It is a time for lying back in God's arms, if even for a moment.

I gather that the literal translation of *Sabbath* is "a time for quieting the heart." At its best and truest, summer is like that, too.

In a letter to a friend, the poet Emily Dickinson confessed that, of all the commandments, "Consider the lilies of the field" is the only one she is sure she never broke. I wish I had her confidence. I don't always consider the lilies. But in the summer, I come close. It begins with crossing items off my to-do list. They can wait, and the lilies cannot.

Prayer

God, help me receive the blessings of this season with a quieted and grateful heart. Amen.

Do This in Remembrance

When he had given thanks, he broke
[the bread], and said, "This is my body that is
for you. Do this in remembrance of me."
—1 Corinthians 11:24

Last month I came across a little notebook with grease-splattered pages about the size of large index cards. On each card is a recipe, written in my mother's warm yet tidy handwriting. My mother died almost twenty years ago, so coming across this notebook was a bit like finding hidden treasure, with a huge helping of poignancy.

This notebook contains all my mother's go-to recipes—Spaghetti Loaf Casserole, Cheese Soufflé Sandwiches, Forgotten Cookies (I almost want to skip the devotional and just give you the recipe for this one—perhaps another time).

This was definitely cooking from another era. The recipes include a lot of canned mushroom soup, mayonnaise, cream, and butter by the tub. Jell-O is well represented. And tiny marshmallows are as well.

Just reading the recipes was enough to unlock memories, but I longed for something more.

So one summer afternoon, I made my mother's Dill Stroganoff. Normally I would cut down on the amount of sour cream, but this time I wanted to make it just as my mother had.

When we sat down to eat, the stroganoff was exactly as I remembered it. The aromas and tastes were transporting. And the stories flowed. It was almost as if my mother were there with us.

The power in Communion is so much more than the power of memory. But when Jesus referred to a common meal and said, "Do this in remembrance of me," at the very least, he meant something like this.

Prayer

Jesus, bless this meal that we are about to share with you. Bless us with your presence. Amen.

I Can't Forgive Myself

If you, O Lord, should mark iniquities, Lord,
who could stand? But there is forgiveness
with you, so that you may be revered.

—from Psalm 130

I often hear people say something along these lines: "I am finding it hard to forgive myself." Hard? How about impossible? As someone once put it, we can no more forgive ourselves than we can sit in our own laps.

What we *can* do is accept the forgiveness of another. Forgiveness is not an achievement. It is always a gift. And that is part of what brings us to worship each week—to receive the gift of God's forgiveness.

Someone I know left the church early in his adolescence, but difficult circumstances in his life prompted him to go back to worship—just to check it out, mind you. He wasn't about to get carried away. He was willing to make a small, tentative step, however. He sat in the back pew so he could observe. But when they came to the prayer of confession and he heard everyone say together, "We have done those things that we ought not to have done and we have left undone those things that we ought to have done," he smiled and said to himself, "Sounds just like my kind of crowd. I came to the right place."

Prayer

Dear God, forgive me, because, try as I might, I am not able to forgive myself. Help me to receive forgiveness as the gift it is. Amen.

Holy Places

> "Surely the Lord is in this place—and I did not know it!"
> And he [Jacob] was afraid, and said,
> "How awesome is this place! This is none other than
> the house of God, and this is the gate of heaven."
> **—from Genesis 28:10–17**

Protestants often pooh-pooh the whole notion of holy places. Other religions, and other traditions within Christianity, have shrines and temples where God's presence is thought to be patently manifest. By contrast, Protestants usually are more comfortable affirming that God can be encountered anywhere, rather than in a particular place.

But I think most Protestants have more of a sense of holy places than we usually let on. For instance, one such place for me is James Chapel at Union Seminary in New York. When I visited there, I felt that I should take off my shoes before treading on such holy ground. My senses were on high alert, trying to take it all in. When I got home, I could barely tell the story of my visit to James Chapel without tearing up. You see, my parents met at Union and they were married in the chapel in 1941.

The high, carved gothic pews are no longer there, as they are in the photographs of my parents on their wedding day. Today James Chapel looks more like a black box theater. But, to me, it is still a holy place because holy things happen there. Oftentimes when I meet Union graduates, I tell them about how James Chapel is a holy place for me.

Then last summer I visited my brother, who has been sorting through old family photos. His collection included a shot of my parents on their wedding day. I was about to tell him about my pilgrimage to James Chapel when I noticed, at the bottom of the photo, this inscription in my mother's handwriting:

"First Methodist Church, Albion, Michigan." (My mother was from Michigan.)

It turns out that, for decades, I simply had the story wrong and my parents, who died years ago, were not around to set me straight.

But when I visit Union Seminary, I will step into James Chapel, and it will still seem like a holy place to me. A holy place is where holy things happen—or, at least, where holy things are remembered, sometimes with tears, and other times with laughter.

Prayer
God, bless all the holy places in my life. Amen.

Your Heart Will Follow

Where your treasure is, there your heart will be also.
—from Matthew 6:19–21

Jesus's statement, "Where your treasure is, there your heart will be also," may sound familiar, but if we don't read it with care, we might reverse the statement through a kind of scriptural dyslexia. We might read it to say, "Where your heart is, there will your treasure be also." That would make sense to us because much of the time our dollars follow our heart's lead. We give to what matters to us. But that isn't what Jesus said.

Think of the appeal you hear over and over again from, say, National Public Radio or your alma mater: If you care about this institution, you will write a check. In other words, "Where your heart is, there will your treasure be also." But Jesus didn't say that.

Jesus is speaking of a different dynamic: Give and spend where you want your heart to be, and then let your heart catch up. Don't just give to those things you care about. Give to the things you want to care about. Ask yourself, "If I were the sort of person I long to be, then what would I do? How would I spend my money?" Then do what you would do if you were that sort of person. Put your treasure where you want your heart to be. And if you do, Jesus says, your heart will go there.

If you want to care more about the kind of car you drive, buy an expensive one. If you want to care more about property values, remodel your house. But if you want to grow in your faith, bring an offering to God. Wherever your treasure is, your heart is sure to follow.

Prayer
O God, fashion my spending and my giving in ways that refashion my heart. Amen.

Eleven Words

The old life is gone; a new life burgeons! Look at
it! All this comes from the God who settled the
relationship between us and him, and then called
us to settle our relationships with each other.
—from 2 Corinthians 5:16–20 MSG

When I was pastor of a congregation, before Thanksgiving I would sometimes ask this question: "Who will be around your table at Thanksgiving, and does that represent any challenges?" The responses were quite remarkable:

"Well, it all depends on if my aunt shows up."

"This year Thanksgiving is with my wife's family, so we'll be fine. But next year we'll be with my family, and that's a whole other story."

"My brother hasn't been with us for Thanksgiving for a long time, so we'll have to see how that goes."

Can you picture that famous Norman Rockwell painting that depicts a large family gathered at a dining room table for a Thanksgiving meal? The father is at the head of the table, hands folded. All heads are bowed. I always assumed they were all offering prayers of thanksgiving for their manifold blessings. But now I wonder if the prayers were more like these:

"Dear God, help me hold my tongue."

"God, everyone is doing real well so far. Don't desert us now."

"Please help us steer clear of political arguments."

When I imagine prayers like that, the depiction of the Norman Rockwell family goes from merely sentimental to something very real and very poignant.

Ira Byock, a professor at Dartmouth Medical School, writes from his experience with dying patients and grieving families about the eleven words that people need to hear in such moments. Then he rightly observes that these eleven words are important to say—and powerful—not just at such critical moments, but at other times and in other circumstances.

Those eleven words are: "Please forgive me. I forgive you. I love you. Thank you."

Prayer

God, bring a spirit of reconciliation to my heart and to my words. Amen.

Here's to Two Old Sinners

Blessed are the merciful, for
they will receive mercy.

—Matthew 5:7

In the mid-1970s, my father and David H. C. Read, a well-known Scottish-American minister, were touring Germany together. In one city David had arranged to meet the man who had been the commandant of the prisoner of war camp in which he was held during World War II. David was a high-ranking officer at the time, so the two men had come to know each other rather well. They had not seen each other for thirty years, however, and David was nervous about how it would go. As a commandant, the German man had not been cruel, but he had been an enemy. So David did not know how either of them would react upon seeing each other again.

They arranged to meet at the hotel where David and my father were staying. David was clear that he wanted to face the man alone, but he asked my father to return an hour or two later, just in case things were not going well.

My father told me that when he left David's room, his friend was straightening his tie, as visibly anxious as a young man going on a first date. But when my father returned to David's room a couple hours later, he found the two men in shirtsleeves, ties off, drinking scotch, engrossed in friendly conversation. When David saw my father, he smiled and asked, "Would you like to join two old sinners for a drink?"

Notice: two sinners. When you are a sinner who knows that you have received mercy, you are better able to extend mercy to another, to do your part in the dynamic flow of mercy received and mercy given.

Prayer

God, help me to take my part in the endless echo of grace by receiving mercy when it is my time to receive, and by granting mercy when it is my turn to give. Amen.

He Had a Wife?

When Jesus entered Peter's house, he saw his mother-in-law in bed with a fever; he touched her hand, and the fever left her, and she got up and began to serve him.

—from Matthew 8:14–17

This healing story in Matthew is so dramatic that we might overlook one intriguing detail. It makes reference to the apostle Peter's mother-in-law.

Wait, Peter was married? That's right. We don't know if others of Jesus's twelve apostles were married, but we know from this verse that Peter was.

That means that the day he dropped his fishing nets to follow Jesus, he also left his wife and the rest of his family.

Before he headed out with Jesus, do you think he said, "Hey, I've got to go home and explain this to my family first"? And, if so, what did he say to explain why he was following this as-yet little-known teacher? And what did his wife say in response? After all, not only would Peter be gone for extended periods, traveling with Jesus all over Galilee, but while he was away the family would not have money coming in from Peter's fishing business.

Most often, when you take on a challenging task or follow a call, other people are making sacrifices so you can do so. They are the behind-the-scenes people—family members, colleagues, or others—who keep the home fires burning, or pick up the odd chore, to make what you do possible.

Is there someone like that in your life? Can you think of a means to thank him or her for easing your way?

Prayer

Dear God, help me recognize those who support me in ways that I might be tempted to overlook. Amen.

Say Thank You

O give thanks to the Lord, for he is good;
for his steadfast love endures for ever.
—from Psalm 107

On Halloween, when young trick-or-treaters come to the door and dip their hands into a big bowl of candy, the adult accompanying them will almost surely remind them, "Say 'thank you.'" And the young voices will echo, "Thank you." It is something of a Halloween litany.

Children need to be reminded to offer thanks because no one is born grateful. Thankfulness does not come naturally to us and sometimes it does not come at all. Rather, thankfulness must be nurtured.

At almost every turn, the authors of the psalms not only invite but also demand that we offer our thanks to God. They understand the irony that it is by continually offering thanks that we can come to be thankful. And, obviously, children are not the only ones whose thanks need to be prompted.

So, day in and day out, in and out of season, offer thanks—perhaps at first to get the feel of it and then, only in time, because you feel it. Likewise, go to worship to offer thanks to God so that you might be nurtured in the ways of thankfulness. Sometimes words of thanks need to be on our lips before they can—by some slow and largely imperceptible process—take up residence in our hearts. As Habitat for Humanity founder Millard Fuller once observed, "More people act themselves into a new way of thinking than think themselves into a new way of acting." And so it can be when we offer thanks.

Prayer
Thank you, God. Thank you, thank you, thank you. Amen.

What I Learned at the Tattooists Convention

The Pharisees and their scribes were complaining
to his disciples, saying, "Why do you eat and
drink with tax collectors and sinners?"
—from Luke 5:29–32

I once participated in a small gathering of pastors and lay leaders charged with considering how our denomination could become a more multiracial and multicultural church. Around the table were African Americans, European Americans, a Native American, a Japanese American, and Latinos and Latinas, as well as folks of different sexual orientations.

We had wonderfully serious and probing discussions about how we could become a more inclusive church that accepts differences and claims a larger unity.

At the same time and in the same hotel, there was a large convention of tattooists. Every corner of the hotel was crammed with tattoo artists. The men wore cutoff T-shirts and the women wore scanty outfits to show off their tattoos. They had tattoos on every imaginable part of their bodies and I am sure on other parts I don't want to imagine. Their bodies were pierced in ways that made even worldly liberals stare.

After we had finished our last discussion, our inclusive group of church leaders opened the door of the packed hotel lounge and, seeing these tattoo artists all together—like moving wallpaper—we simply closed the door. One member of our group said with a laugh, "You know, it's one thing to be open to differences, but I'm not sure I'm ready to drink with a crowd of tattoo artists."

Since then I've wondered if we might have learned more about being an inclusive church if we had abandoned our polite and careful discussions around the conference table and instead had spent the day hanging out in the lounge with the tattooists.

After all, when we opened the door to that lounge, we didn't look around long enough to see if Jesus was there. And Jesus was criticized for eating and drinking in just such a place.

Prayer

God, open my heart and mind so that I might see who you are calling me to eat and drink with. Amen.

Death and Life in a
Small New Hampshire Church

Pray for one another, that you may be healed.

—James 5:16 ESV

My cousin Pam lived alone on a small New Hampshire farm she inherited from her parents. We did not see each other often, but the contours of her face and particularly the cadence of her voice were such that you wouldn't need a DNA test to know we are related.

Another cousin told me that Pam's cancer had recurred and death was near. *How sad*, I thought, *to approach death alone*. It can be challenging to live alone, I imagined, but it would be far worse to die alone. So I got in my car and wended my way through the serpentine roads of New Hampshire.

When I got near the little town of Hebron, New Hampshire, the GPS quit. This was one place it did not recognize. So I stopped at the small Congregational church, where I interrupted a Bible study, and asked if anyone knew where Pam Yinger lived. They all did. One member of the group accompanied me to my car to point out the road I should take.

When I got to Pam's house, the driveway was clogged with cars. Inside there was a gentle hum of activity. I was greeted by my cousin Michael. A woman was making tea. A few others just seemed to be hanging out. It had the familiar feel of a church potluck. One of them took me to see Pam in the living room, which was festooned with more trinkets than any flea market.

Pam and I chatted a bit. I learned that, other than my cousin Michael, the people in the house were all from the church. They took turns throughout the day and night so she would be cared for around the clock. Before I left, this small handful of God's people, in a land that the GPS forgot, held hands with Pam and one another and we prayed. After I said, "Amen," Pam added her own, "Thank you, dears."

Pam died two days later.

They say the church is dying. Don't you believe it.

Prayer

God, thank you that, in the presence of death, you breathe life. Amen.

What's to Become of the Double-Minded?

I hate the double-minded.

—Psalm 119:113

"I am of two minds on that," we often say in a situation that is difficult to assess or when the correct course of action is not yet clear. So we respond to the words of the poet Robert Frost in his famous poem "The Road Not Taken":

> *Two roads diverged in a yellow wood,*
> *And sorry I could not travel both . . .*

We admire people who pause at a fork in the road. Oftentimes they are the ones who are able to see both sides of an issue and know how to weigh options.

So why does the writer of this psalm envision God saying, "I hate the double-minded"? What's so wrong with being of two minds?

Nothing is wrong with being double-minded in the time before making a decision. But, sooner or later, commitment is called for. You cannot plow a field by turning it over in your mind. Eventually, it comes time to act. As the author Albert Camus observed, sometimes we must make a 100 percent commitment to something about which we are only 51 percent certain.

The perpetually double-minded never get very far from home because they get stuck at the first fork in the road. For them—for all of us, at one time or another—it is best to heed the advice of Yogi Berra: "When you get to a fork in the road, take it."

Prayer

O God, meet me at the crossroads. Show me the way I am to go. Then give me the courage to act. Amen.

My Soul Magnifies

My soul magnifies the Lord, and my spirit
rejoices in God my Savior, for he has looked
with favor on the lowliness of his servant.
—from Luke 1:46–55

In response to the news that she is to give birth to the "Son of the Most High," Mary sings, "My soul magnifies the Lord."

But how can Mary's soul magnify the Lord? The word *magnify* means to make something greater or larger. So how can Mary's soul—or any soul, or anything else, for that matter—make the Lord greater or larger than the Lord already is?

In the Monty Python film *The Meaning of Life*, an Anglican priest leads his congregation in a litany: "O, Lord, you are so big." The congregation responds: "You are so big." "You are so absolutely huge." The congregation echoes: "You are so absolutely huge."

It is a send-up of the psalms, which frequently express awe before the majesty, the greatness, and, indeed, the enormity of God.

Most of the songs of praise found in the Bible are meant to make us feel small. So how can Mary speak of magnifying the Lord? It is not an expression of Mary's pride. It is an expression of her awe.

Mary reminds us through her song that our God demonstrates greatness by being at work in powerful ways through one of the powerless ones. The Lord is enlarged by working through one of the small ones—small, at least, as the world measures things.

Mary understands that God is at work in unexpected places, in the life of a simple country girl, and from her we are reminded that God may be at work in perhaps the most unexpected place of all—our own small lives. And, in that realization, this great God seems even greater, enlarged by the wild miracle of it.

Prayer

God, help me recognize the ways in which your greatness can be manifest in my life. That is, may my own soul magnify you. Amen.

What You Cannot Expect
When You Are Expecting

For God so loved the world that God gave
God's only son, so that everyone who
believes in him might have eternal life.
—John 3:16 AUTHOR'S ADAPTATION

The word *expecting* is a funny expression to use in reference to pregnancy, particularly pregnancy with a first child, because there is so much that you cannot expect. You cannot expect what the child's gifts or temperament will be. You cannot expect how much your life will instantly and permanently change. You cannot expect fully how much you will love this new being.

And, in my experience, you cannot expect how much having a child makes you feel vulnerable to the hurts of the world. Before our children were born, the world and the people in it seemed to have limited power to hurt me. I faced risks with a certain equanimity. After all, what's the worst that could happen?

That changed when I became a parent. My protective love for my children suddenly made me feel, through them, quite vulnerable to the hurts of the world. Through the eyes of a protective parent, I began to see all the ways someone can be hurt—by hot words or frozen silences, by little betrayals, by loneliness, failure, rejection, and disappointment, not to mention injury, disease, and death. The world seemed like a much more threatening place than it had before. That's because, when you have children, it's like your own naked and vulnerable heart has been sent out into the world. And, as much as we may try, our ability to protect our children is so very limited.

And that is how I understand—still dimly, but at an almost visceral level—what it means to affirm that God sent God's own son into the world. That is, in Jesus, God sent God's own naked and vulnerable heart into the world.

Prayer

Thank you, God, for loving us so much that you were willing to make yourself vulnerable for our sakes. Amen.

Praising God and Enjoying God

Sing to God, sing praises to [God's] name.
—from Psalm 68:4–10

Once while leading a group of teenagers in a Bible study, I asked for responses to a psalm of praise, and one girl said, with a disgusted wrinkle of her nose, "Such an ego!" When I asked what she meant, she replied, "I mean, if you know you're God, why do you have to be told how great you are all the time?"

Good question.

I have concluded that God invites our praise not because God needs our praise, but because we need to praise God. For one, praise puts us in our place. Our place is not at the center of the universe. That is God's place. As someone once said to me, "Have you noticed how crowded it can get at the center of the universe? At least that's what I find every time I try to elbow my way in there." Praise is a way of stepping back from the center of the universe.

Then, too, the praise of God is a delight. To praise God is to enjoy God.

The first question in a historic catechism is this: What is the chief end of human life? The answer: To glorify God and enjoy God forever. And one of the ways in which we enjoy God is to praise God. Worship that is full of praise is infused with joy. That is, in praise-filled worship it may seem as if we are enjoying ourselves, but actually we are enjoying God. What a delightful, delicious notion that is.

Prayer

Great God, I praise your name. May I delight in glorifying you and enjoy you forever. Amen.

Jesus's Packing Instructions

Take no gold, or silver, or copper in your belts, no
bag for your journey, or two tunics, or sandals,
or a staff; for laborers deserve their food.

—from Matthew 10:5–15

People have different philosophies of packing.

Some like to travel light. They take a bare minimum of items with them. They count the number of days they will be away and bring just that many pairs of socks—no more, no less.

Others have an "in case" attitude toward packing. They might pack a raincoat, a down parka, and a bathing suit just in case the weather changes.

Clearly, Jesus is in the former category. In fact, he is the ultimate light packer. When sending his disciples on their first journey without him, he gives very explicit packing instructions: Don't take any money or a change of clothes. In fact, leave your suitcase home. Don't take anything but the shirt on your back.

Talk about traveling light! What is Jesus up to here?

Perhaps Jesus gives this advice so his disciples will learn trust. It is Jesus's way of encouraging them to engage with the people they meet. After all, when you don't have enough to go on, you have to turn to those around you.

But there is another possible explanation. The items Jesus tells his disciples to leave behind are just the kinds of things that worshipers were told to leave outside the temple before they entered. People were to divest themselves of these things before stepping on holy ground.

So when Jesus tells his disciples to travel light, he is encouraging them to approach the whole world as if it were holy ground, a place where you could expect to encounter God.

What would it mean for you to enter your day in this way?

Prayer

God, send me into this day inspired to see the holy in the everyday. Amen.

"Didn't I Wash Your Feet?"

> Then he poured water into a basin and began to
> wash the disciples' feet and to wipe them with
> the towel that was tied around him. . . . Peter
> said to him, "You will never wash my feet."
> —from John 13:1–17

A parishioner in my former congregation tells about a conversation she had in a small store near the church. She saw a man who looked vaguely familiar and asked, "Didn't I wash your feet last Thursday?" The man responded, "I think so, but it was rather dark, so I can't be sure."

She went on: "I had never done anything like that before. That's why I was so nervous."

"Well, it was a first for me, also."

Then they became aware that the shopkeeper behind the counter looked both shocked and confused by what she was hearing. Seeing this reaction, my parishioner rushed to reassure the shopkeeper: "It's not like it sounds. We are both part of Village Church. We do that kind of thing there." Still aghast, the shopkeeper laughed nervously and then abruptly changed the subject.

It is good to know that Jesus's followers are still capable of shocking others by their outrageous behavior. After all, we are following a master who consistently shocked others by doing outrageous things—like washing his disciples' feet, a servant's task.

It has been customary through the centuries for the Pope to commemorate Jesus washing the feet of his disciples by washing the feet of twelve priests at the Vatican each Holy Thursday. Over time, it wasn't shocking anymore, but more like a beloved ritual.

Then along comes Pope Francis, who washes the feet of priests, yes, but also women, prisoners, Muslims, people with disabilities. Many were horrified by his outrageous behavior. Others, like me, rejoice that a simple act of servant leadership still has the power to shock and inspire.

Prayer

Jesus, help me confound others' expectations—even my own—through surprising acts of love. Amen.

How Can I Keep from Singing?

About midnight Paul and Silas were
praying and singing hymns to God, and
the prisoners were listening to them.

—from Acts 16:25–32

Paul and Silas are in Philippi to tell the story of Jesus when they are accused of disturbing the peace. So they are badly beaten and thrown in jail. But notice how they react to the chains, the bruised limbs, the undoing of their plans: They hold choir practice. They sing.

Would you sing under those circumstances? Paul and Silas can sing because they feel embraced by the love of God that can reach into any place and circumstance. They sing the story of Jesus, the one who entered the dark corners and prisons of our lives so that we might join him in his freedom and victory.

A few years ago, a Greek cruise ship sank off the coast of South Africa. After the ship ran aground, the crew, with a few passengers, deserted the vessel in lifeboats. The remaining passengers were brought together to await rescue helicopters. There the ship's entertainers tried to keep gloom at bay with magic tricks, jokes, and sing-alongs. One passenger later recalled, "There we were, sitting in the dark, singing songs to keep our minds off the cold and fright. We began with 'We Are Sailing,' but decided that it wasn't true. We got into 'My Bonnie Lies Over the Ocean' and 'Good-bye Love, Good-bye Happiness,' but this did nothing for morale."

Eventually, all the passengers were saved before the ocean consumed the ship. But I wonder if, since that experience, any of the passengers have searched for other songs to sing, other stories to live by, amid the threatening storms that are sure to return.

That seems to me to be a good test of the songs we sing and the stories we choose to live by: Can I take it to prison with me? Or to a sinking ship? Would it sustain me even then?

Prayer

O God, in the words of the old hymn, "Through all the tumult and the strife, I hear the music ringing; it finds an echo in my soul, how can I keep from singing?" Amen.

Keep the Paradox

Can you find out the deep
things of God? Can you find out
the limit of the Almighty?

—Job 11:7

When Howard Dean ran for president in 2004, he was asked to name his favorite book of the New Testament. He replied, "The book of Job." I winced a bit at his reply. You see, for nine years I was Howard's pastor. His mistake almost seemed like grounds for a clergy malpractice suit (he says, while also invoking the statute of limitations).

But I have to stand with Howard. I love the book of Job, particularly for the ways it consistently affirms the utter incomprehensibility of God, as when Job's friend Zophar challenges him with a series of unanswerable questions:

Can you find out the deep things of God?
Can you find out the limit of the Almighty?
It is higher than heaven—what can you do?
Deeper than Sheol—what can you know?

In the New Testament, we meet the same God, but in a close and intimate way. In Jesus, the distant and majestic creator of the heavens and the earth becomes Emmanuel, that is, "God with us." He is as close as our own lives, as familiar as the way home and yet also, at the same time, the fullest expression of God's power and glory.

There may be two testaments, but there is only one God—the God of majesty and intimacy, the God who, in the words of a Communion liturgy, is as "close to us as breathing and distant as the farthest star."

No matter how much of the Bible you remember or forget, keep that paradox intact and you will know much of what is important to know about our God.

Prayer

O God, ever close and ever distant, give me the patience—and the faith—to hold tight to paradoxes. Amen.

Fresh Notebooks

Clean the slate, God, so we can start the day fresh!
—**Psalm 19:13 MSG**

When I was young, I loved anticipating the first day of school. On the night before that first day, I would study the roster of my class as if it were holy writ and fantasize that many of the classmates I did not yet know would all soon become good friends. I would lay out my clothes on the floor just right (the socks already in the shoes, for instance), as if I expected that the next morning I would be able to jump into them in a single acrobatic movement.

What I loved most, however, were the new notebooks. They always seemed so fresh and full of promise. They didn't contain a single misspelled word or grammatical error. There were no incorrect calculations; there was no indecipherable handwriting. There was nothing in them at all. This is what I found so appealing. Clean notebooks were the epitome of the fresh start. Whatever mistakes I had made in the past were, indeed, in the past, and I could start anew. I found that reassuring and even close to thrilling, as only a new start can be.

I have often heard people say they don't like prayers of confession in worship. To them, prayers of confession feel like a downer. That is not my experience. To me such prayers, particularly when followed by an assurance of pardon, are like being handed a new notebook before the first day of school. It is a clean slate, a fresh start. To me, that is not only reassuring—it can be thrilling.

Prayer
Clean my slate, God, so I can start afresh. Amen.

A Mere Tip of the Hat

The kingdom of heaven is like a mustard seed that someone took and sowed in his field; it is the smallest of all the seeds, but when it has grown it is the greatest of shrubs and becomes a tree, so that the birds of the air come and make nests in its branches.

—from Matthew 13:31–33

In his memoirs, nineteenth-century author Oscar Wilde recalled an experience while he was in prison, where he was held after being declared—in the strange manner of his day—"guilty" of homosexuality. He writes: "When I was brought down from my prison . . . between two policemen, [a man I know] waited in the long dreary corridor so that, before the whole crowd, whom an action so sweet and simple hushed into silence, he might gravely raise his hat to me as, handcuffed and with bowed head, I passed him by. Men have gone to heaven for smaller things than that."

After Episcopal Archbishop Desmond Tutu won a Nobel Peace Prize for his nonviolent struggle against apartheid in South Africa, he was asked to recall the formative experiences of his life. He replied, "One incident comes to mind immediately. When I was a young child, I saw a man tip his hat to a black woman. Please understand that such a gesture is completely unheard of in my country. The white man was an Episcopal bishop and the black woman was my mother."

These two stories remind me that even a small, fragile gesture can take on grand dimensions when it is offered in love. Our own efforts may be small, but through them the largest of all realities—the love of God—can be communicated. A mere tip of the hat can offer hope and change a life.

Prayer
God, remind me not to neglect small acts of compassion so that you, in turn, might fill them with your great love. Amen.

The Serious Business of Joy

Then the disciples of John came to him, saying, "Why do we and the Pharisees fast often, but your disciples do not fast?" And Jesus said to them, "The wedding guests cannot mourn as long as the bridegroom is with them, can they?"

—Matthew 9:14–15

Billy Sunday, a famous evangelist of the early twentieth century, observed, "The trouble with many people is that they have got just enough religion to make them miserable." They are serious about their religion (which is a good thing) but in a dour way (which is not). They know a good deal about duty, but grace is a stranger to them. Their confessions are long, and their minds wander during the assurance of pardon. Billy Sunday concluded, "If you have no joy in your religion, there's a leak in your faith."

Some critics of Jesus thought he had the opposite problem—he was too joyful. Jesus and his followers did not fast as often as others did. In fact, Jesus relished food and drink so much that some accused him of being a glutton and a drunkard. Beyond that, Jesus just seemed to be having too good a time. There's got to be something wrong with that, or so concluded some of his contemporaries.

When the good religious folk ("Good in the worst sense of the word," as Mark Twain put it) confronted Jesus about this, he likened himself to the groom at a wedding celebration. You cannot expect a groom to be anything but joyful. A groom is supposed to be joyful, and there is something amiss if he is not. And those celebrating the wedding are expected to, well, celebrate.

C. S. Lewis once affirmed that "Joy is the serious business of heaven." Jesus obviously thought joy is the serious business of the living as well.

Prayer

God, repair any leaks in my faith by giving me the gift of joy. Amen.

Epiphanies at the Dump

Have dominion over the fish of the sea and
over the birds of the air and over every
living thing that moves upon the earth.

—from Genesis 1

For twenty years, I lived in a town that took great pride in the local dump. It was officially known as the Recycling and Disposal Facility, but everyone called it "the Dump." In some respects, the Dump is the center of the town, something like the town green. It is where politicians come to make their pitches, public advocates get their petitions signed, and Girl Scouts sell their cookies.

Everyone goes to the Dump. Hardly anyone in our town has their trash collected curbside. That would be considered irresponsible, if not downright gauche.

At the Dump, there are at least thirty different categories of recyclables, each with its own bin, so sorting provides ample opportunity for reflection.

I used to wonder why our town doesn't pick up trash and recyclables curbside. After all, it can't be good for the environment to have a lineup of SUVs all waiting to get to the Dump, then idling while trash is deposited.

Nevertheless, I have concluded that it is good that we are expected to bring our own trash to the Dump. If someone explains how many parts per million of carbon dioxide is dangerous for human life, I will mostly understand what is being said, and I will appreciate the urgency on an intellectual basis. For me, however, none of that brings home the crisis of the environment quite like loading up my car and taking trash and recyclables to the Dump. It is not just a chance to see some people I know. It is also an opportunity like none other to see myself and my consuming ways. So when I drive away, I sometimes offer a prayer of confession.

Prayer

God, hear my confession: Oftentimes, I consume the world's resources as if the earth were my own rather than yours. Give me a renewed sense that I am a steward of your creation. Amen.

Yes

In him every one of God's promises is a "Yes."
For this reason it is through him that we
say the "Amen," to the glory of God.
—from 2 Corinthians 1:15–22

A while back I was asked to summarize the gospel in seven words or less. Here is what I came up with: "God gets the last word."

If I were asked to summarize the gospel in just one word, however, it would be the word *yes*. The apostle Paul affirmed that, in Jesus, "It is always 'Yes.' For in him every one of God's promises is a 'Yes.'"

There is a famous book on negotiation called *Getting to Yes*. That could be the title for the gospel story as well because, in Jesus, God always gets to yes.

During Jesus's lifetime, the human family used every way we knew to say no to him. We rejected him, betrayed him, denied him, killed him. And yet, in the resurrection, God would not take our no for an answer. Before and after and under our definite no is God's triumphant yes.

As the poet Wallace Stevens wrote, "After the final no there comes a yes, and on that yes the future world depends."

So God gets the last word. And that last word is *yes*.

Prayer

*i thank you God for most this amazing
day: for the leaping greenly spirits of trees
and a blue true dream of sky; and for everything
which is natural which is infinite which is yes.*

—E. E. Cummings

Finish the Story

So they went out and fled from the tomb, for
terror and amazement had seized them; and they
said nothing to anyone, for they were afraid.
—from Mark 16:1–8

My favorite feature of the children's magazines of my childhood were the stories that brought the reader to the climax of the story, to the very edge of adventure, and then stopped abruptly with this instruction: "Finish the story." If the story was a good one, my mind would wander in great frontiers of thought.

In one grade-school class, the teacher asked us to write our own ending to *Charlotte's Web*. I remember writing so furiously that I had to go up to the teacher's desk for my twelfth piece of paper (this is not an approximation). That's what can happen when you start with a story that captures the imagination. It can open up new and great possibilities, sending our minds in larger orbits than they might otherwise occupy.

Today's scripture verse is the last verse in Mark's Gospel. But the story he tells is not finished. It awaits people who hear the story and resolve to see it to its completion.

The story of Jesus is not completed through words, of course, but through our lives. We can determine through our actions if the story of Jesus will end up as a mere history lesson or romantic fantasy. Or, with even just a sliver of faith, if it will be a continuing adventure that not only sends out thoughts in directions both grand and noble, but sends our lives in those directions, too.

How are you going to help finish the story today?

Prayer
Jesus, I am grateful your story continues in our time and sometimes—unlikely miracle that it is—through me. Amen.

Still the Same Old Story

As Paul and Barnabas were going out, the people urged
them to speak about these things again the next sabbath.
—from Acts 13:26–42

When our daughter, Alanna, was still a young girl, she already
had a shelf full of books in her room. At bedtime, I would ask
her to pick out the book she would like me to read to her. Most
often she would not pick out a new book, but instead one of
her favorites, like *Goodnight Moon*.

I would read, "In the great green room there was a telephone and a red balloon and a picture of the cow jumping over
the moon . . ." And when I reached the end of the story, Alanna
would always say, "Again!"

Just tell it again. The same old story is enough.

When we are older, we tire of most stories after the first
few readings. But there is one story we do not tire of, because it
stirs something in us each time. It's the story of God's fierce love
affair with the world, known first in God's relationship with
the people of Israel and then through Jesus Christ. We can no
more tire of it than we can tire of the words *I love you*, which,
of course, is just the message this story brings: God's love made
known to us.

Paul told this same story in his sermon to the people of
Antioch. So as they shook hands with Paul at the door after
worship, they asked him to tell the same story the following
week. Again! Just tell it again.

Prayer
God, thank you for the old, old story of your love for me and for
all humankind. Amen.

Habits

They came to Thessalonica, where there was a synagogue
of the Jews. And Paul went in, as was his custom.

—Acts 17:1–2

The apostle Paul went to the synagogue in Thessalonica "as was his custom." In other words, it was his habit. If you do something out of habit, you don't exactly decide to do it. You just do it.

When it comes to leading a moral life, we tend to emphasize the decisions a person makes. But in such matters, habits are even more important than decisions. Aristotle, the great Greek philosopher, wrote, "We are what we repeatedly do."

We all need habits because we can't think about everything. If I had to decide each day if I was going to eat three meals, brush my teeth, dress in the morning, go to work, go home at night—if I had to decide to do all those things every day—it would be exhausting. We cannot live happily with so many decisions. So we have habits.

Aristotle also wrote, "Moral excellence comes about as a result of habit. We become just by doing just acts, temperate by doing temperate acts, brave by doing brave acts."

That's why Jesus is so focused not on how we think or feel but on how we act. Give your shirt. Turn the other cheek. Pray for those who persecute you. Do this in remembrance of me. You don't need to think about it. Just do it. If you do these things over and over again, they will become habits. They will become who you are.

Prayer
God, I have many habits. Help me adopt some good ones. Amen.

The Power in Blessing

The Lord bless you and keep you; the Lord make his face
to shine upon you, and be gracious to you; the Lord lift
up his countenance upon you, and give you peace.

—from Numbers 6:22–27

There is great power in the act of blessing. So why don't we offer more blessings for one another?

We may assume the people we care about don't need a blessing. We think our children need advice. We see that our parents need support. A friend needs a listening ear. A spouse needs a kind word. Someone who has annoyed me needs a piece of my mind. We may not consider that what someone may need more than anything else—what that person may be hungry for, in some cases dying of hunger for—is a blessing.

Or we may have concluded that someone doesn't deserve a blessing. There is an old Gaelic blessing: "May those who love us love us. And those who don't, may they turn their hearts; and for those who don't turn their hearts, may they turn their ankles, so we'll know them by their limping."

Doesn't that capture the kind of blessings we are sometimes tempted to offer? It's more like a curse—which, of course, is the opposite of a blessing. Sometimes the good words stick on our tongues.

So it's important to remember that words of blessing are borrowed words. We are asking God to bless because we may not have any good words of our own to offer. To say "May God bless you" is to borrow the power of God to offer good words when that seems beyond us. It is asking God to take the lead.

Prayer

God, bless those I would like to bless, and those I am unable to bless on my own. Amen.

The Sin of Holding Coats

Then they dragged [Stephen] out of the city and
began to stone him; and the witnesses laid their
coats at the feet of a young man named Saul.

—from Acts 7:51–8:1

This is a disturbing story about the stoning of Stephen, the first deacon. His offense? Testifying to the love of Jesus. And for that, the mob dragged Stephen out of town and began to stone him to death. But before they had finished the job, they took off their coats, presumably so they could really go at it. They laid their coats at the feet of a young man named Saul for safekeeping. (After his conversion, his name became Paul, to mark the dramatic change in his life.)

Obviously, killing another human being is a terrible sin, but so is standing by in silence when a wrong is being committed. Perhaps no one reading this has ever killed anyone, but silence in the face of violence or injustice is a sin of which all of us are guilty.

As the Nazis rose to political power, a German pastor, Martin Niemoller, famously said, "First they came for the communists, and I did not speak out—because I am not a communist. Then they came for the socialists, and I did not speak out—because I am not a socialist. Then they came for the trade unionists, and I did not speak out—because I am not a trade unionist. Then they came for the Jews, and I did not speak out—because I am not a Jew. Then they came for me—and there was no one left to speak out for me."

Prayer
My prayer today is a silent prayer . . . of confession. Amen.

Get Fired Up!

So, because you are lukewarm, and
neither cold nor hot, I am about
to spit you out of my mouth.
—from Revelation 3:15–22

For a moment, imagine with John, the author of Revelation, that it is the end of the age and you have been brought before the judgment seat. What do you most fear might be revealed about your life? That you denied the existence of God? That you disobeyed God?

John imagines that the most egregious sin is being lukewarm in our devotion to God. He goes on to imagine that it would be better to turn a cold shoulder to God, to have our relationship with God freeze over entirely, than for us to be tepid in our devotion to God.

At first, this may surprise us. It doesn't seem as if being lukewarm could be so bad. In relationships, however, the opposite of love is not hate, but rather something more like lukewarm indifference.

This can be the same in our relationship with God. Those who rail against God, or actively doubt God, or even knowingly disobey God, at least accord God a considerable role in their lives. At least such a person is not indifferent or casual or dull. There is room for growth in such a person, which is another way of saying that there is room for God.

C. S. Lewis once wrote: "Christianity . . . if false, is of *no* importance, and if true, of infinite importance. The one thing it cannot be is moderately important." A lukewarm Christian tries to make of Christianity something moderately important. But Christ inspires and requires so much more. The only appropriate response is to get fired up.

Prayer

God of Pentecost fire, do not let me settle into being lukewarm in my devotion to you. Amen.

Cheerful Givers

God loves a cheerful giver.
—from 2 Corinthians 9:6–15

"God loves a cheerful giver," says the apostle Paul. But is there any other kind? In my experience givers *are* cheerful. I have never known any truly giving person who has not been a person of cheer. Joy is one of the indelible characteristics of the giving person.

I am not referring to the kind of reluctant, sharp-penciled, let-me-figure-out-what-my-share-is kind of giver. Rather, I am thinking of the openhanded, openhearted givers. They not only spread cheer and share joy, they obviously *know* cheer and *experience* joy.

We might wonder which comes first: Do these people know cheer and joy because they are givers, or are they givers because they are people of cheer and joy? The question seems strangely moot, however, for in the lives of such people the two are inextricably intertwined. Joy and giving flow from one another in a sure and blessed way. Think of it as the endless echo of grace.

Among the reasons givers are cheerful is that, in giving to others, we are acting in accordance with God's intentions for our lives. After all, we are created to be givers, meant to be givers. So when we close in on ourselves in self-concern, we are departing from what God intends for us, and there is no joy in that.

So Paul enjoins us to give, to borrow the words of Jesus, "so that my joy may be in you, and that your joy may be complete" (John 15:11).

Prayer
God, help me take my part in an echo of grace, where giving and joy flow from one another. Amen.

Staying Close to the Water

Jesus said to her, "Everyone who drinks of
this water will be thirsty again, but those
who drink of the water that I will give
them will never be thirsty. The water that
I will give will become in them a spring
of water gushing up to eternal life."
—from John 4:7–15

The daughter of a dear friend of mine spent some time working at a huge cattle ranch in the Australian outback. The land is so vast and arid that the ranchers don't rely on fences to keep the cattle from wandering off. What keeps the cattle around instead is a deep well of pure water. Cows may not be the smartest of creatures, but they soon learn that you don't want to wander too far from the well.

This seems like an apt metaphor for a particular approach to the Christian faith. There are traditions that rely on something like fences to keep some in and to keep others out. They might say you have to believe in a particular creed to belong, or you have to have some kind of dramatic conversion experience to be one of us.

There are others—and I am one—who do not approach the Christian faith in that way. We are not big on fences and, in fact, we don't think they are needed.

Instead, we focus on the well and the life-giving water that can be found there. We have our center in the gospel of Jesus Christ. To be sure, we have our different understandings of the gospel, and some of us might even wander far afield, but we don't construct fences. That's because we trust that the well is enough—it is more than enough—to keep us close.

Prayer

Thank you, God, for the living water that keeps us alive and refreshes our spirits. Help us stay close to the source of that water this day and in the days to come. Amen.

What's an Hour?

Could you not keep watch for one hour?
—from Mark 14:32–42 NASB

Jesus was upset with his most trusted disciples because they could not stay awake for an hour while he prayed. After all, what's an hour?

Well, it depends . . .

An hour taking a test feels like a breathless sprint. An hour waiting in line seems to plod along on leaden feet.

An hour spent waiting for the parade to come down the street is full of eager anticipation. An hour waiting in the doctor's office to hear about test results may be full of dread.

An hour can breeze by, or it can feel like a great weight on your chest.

An hour can be hard. Sometimes we are not up to the challenges of an hour. Sometimes an hour is more than we can bear.

But, to be honest, to watch for one hour while Jesus prays doesn't seem like that much of a challenge, does it? Other hours carry much greater challenges than that.

Which may be why the disciples weren't up to it. Sometimes it is the little tasks we just can't find the energy to carry out. Sometimes it's easier to rise to a larger challenge. It gets our attention. We dig down deep. Oftentimes, the bigger challenge draws the best from us.

Waiting one hour while Jesus prays just doesn't seem all that difficult—which may be why the disciples were not able to pull it off.

Prayer
God, I frequently ask you to help me in the times of my biggest challenges, but today I seek your help with the smaller challenges that I am used to addressing on my own. Amen.

Thanks

Rejoice always, pray without ceasing,
give thanks in all circumstances.

—from 1 Thessalonians 5:12–21

The closest I have ever come to meeting royalty is when my wife, Karen, and I were invited to a reception for the great jazz singer Ella Fitzgerald. The reception was being held after her concert in the small city where we lived at the time. I love jazz and I have always adored Ella Fitzgerald. So I eagerly looked forward to the concert and was thrilled at the prospect of meeting her.

I no longer remember what I had intended to say to her when I had my chance to shake her hand. I am sure I rehearsed something. I probably planned to say something I thought was witty or that she might remember. But when I extended my hand to shake hers, I not only couldn't remember what I intended to say, I couldn't think of anything to say. I was speechless. I had my moment, but I had no words. Then, eventually, still shaking her hand, with a bit of a stammer, I said, "Thank you so much, Miss Fitzgerald." That is all I could say.

In response, she just gave a sweet, shy little smile and nodded her head. That was it. But somehow, it was enough. As the great medieval theologian and mystic Meister Eckhart once observed, "If the only prayer you say in your entire life is 'Thank you,' it will be enough."

Prayer

Thank you, thank you, thank you. Is that really enough? Thank you. Amen.

You Got Rhythm?

For everything there is a season, and a time
for every matter under heaven.
—from Ecclesiastes 3:1–8

Everyone is talking about balance these days. We want more balance in our lives. We complain about the lack of balance. We strive for the right balance between our work lives and the rest of our lives. Magazines provide carefully balanced lists of suggestions about how to get more balance. But, frankly, to me the whole concept of balance sounds exhausting, like balancing on one foot or balancing a tray of full glasses while walking on a rocky path—I can do it, to be sure, but not for long. I don't know of anyone who can stay balanced for very long.

But balance is not a biblical virtue. Instead, the way of life that is commended in the Bible is more about rhythm than it is about balance. There is the rhythm of the week, six days of work and one day of rest, set within the larger rhythms of the liturgical year. Jesus spent time in intense engagement with the people around him alternating in rhythm with time alone or with close friends. And then there is the basic spiritual rhythm of breathing in and breathing out. Indeed, there is "a time for every matter under heaven," which is an ancient affirmation of the place of rhythm in our lives.

When we strive for balance, it is like standing on one foot. When we respond to the rhythms of creation, it is more like taking part in a dance—first one foot, and then the other. Which one sounds more life-giving to you?

Prayer

God, help me know how to move my feet in the rhythmic dance of your creation, first one and then the other. And if I lose my balance, help me pick myself up, dust myself off, and start all over again. Amen.

Watch Your Feet

A man had two sons; he went to the first and
said, "Son, go and work in the vineyard today." He
answered, "I will not"; but later he changed his mind
and went. The father went to the second and said
the same; and he answered, "I go, sir"; but he did not
go. Which of the two did the will of his father?

—from Matthew 21:23–32

Saint Jerome described the person of faith as the one in whom the heart, the feet, and the mouth all agree. Or, to use an expression that is common in some church circles, "You can't just talk the talk, you've also got to walk the walk." We expect words and actions to be consistent.

In this parable, however, Jesus imagines two sons who are both inconsistent. One doesn't say all the right things but does just what he is supposed to do. The other son says all the right things but does nothing. Jesus is clear about which is preferable: He praises the one who walks the walk, even when he doesn't talk the talk.

Here Jesus is telling us something we may know already, but we still need to be reminded of on a regular basis. Words alone—even when they are all the right words—are not enough. In the end, it is actions that matter. After all, it is not a compliment to say of someone, "He is all talk and no action." But it is a high compliment, indeed, when it is said of someone, "She is a person of action and very few words."

As the novelist and preacher Frederick Buechner observed, "If you want to know who you really are as distinct from who you like to think you are, keep an eye on where your feet take you."

Where are your feet taking you today?

Prayer

Dear God, guide my feet today to where I need to be or to where I am needed. Amen.

Love Endures

Love . . . bears all things, believes all things,
hopes all things, endures all things.
—from 1 Corinthians 13:1–8

In his famous hymn to love, the apostle Paul says that love "endures all things." Endurance is not one of the sexier spiritual virtues. It sounds like a lot of work, and not always pleasant work at that.

By comparison, faith can sound glamorous. After all, you can make a leap of faith. A leap! Why, it's almost dashing. Love sounds grand. There are songs written about love. In fact, it's hard to find a song that isn't written about love. Courage sounds gallant. Hope sounds, well . . . hopeful.

And endurance? It doesn't sound glamorous or grand or gallant. It just sounds like a lot of work.

I have come to think of endurance, however, as love with its work clothes on. When Paul says, "Love bears all things . . . endures all things," it is another way of saying that love endures because it puts up with a lot.

A while back, I was talking with someone who was reflecting on the challenge of relating on an ongoing basis with a person who is particularly difficult. "It's an endurance test. That's what it is like to be her friend—it's an endurance test." *What a great description*, I thought. After all, to *endure* means two different things—"to put up with a lot" "and to last." Two different meanings, and yet, when love has its work clothes on, the two are inextricably related. Love *endures* all things.

Prayer
Thank you, God, that there are people whose love for me endures. In some ways they put up with a lot, but that also means that their love for me is lasting. What a gift. Amen.

An Awkward Christmas

Mary said to the angel, "How can this be,
since I am a virgin?"
—from Luke 1:26–38

Even the best-rehearsed Christmas pageants display a certain awkwardness. In one pageant at our church, when Mary was visited by the angel Gabriel and told that she would give birth to the "Son of the Most High," the little girl who played Mary said in a loud, clear voice, "How can this be, since I have no husband?" The girl playing the angel, responding to some unrehearsed reflex, gave a shrug, as if to say, "Beats me, Mary. I'm just the messenger."

If there is a certain awkwardness in Christmas pageants, that may be because they reflect the awkwardness of the event they aim to depict. How shall people play their parts in this drama? There is no familiar or predictable script to follow. Mary must be both the mother of the baby Jesus and, at the same time, the child of Jesus, who is Lord of us all. The shepherds, who know how to behave in a stable, know nothing about how to behave around a king. The Magi, who know how to behave around a king, know nothing about what to do in a stable.

And no one knows what to expect next. After all, if the Lord of the universe is born in such an unlikely place, far from glamour and fanfare, in the kind of places we spend our own days, then God could show up anywhere.

Prayer
God, I know you appear in the most unlikely places. Help me see the ways in which you are at work in perhaps the most unlikely place of all—my own life. Amen.

The Eyes of the Heart Enlightened

> I pray that the God of our Lord Jesus Christ, the
> Father of glory, may give you a spirit of wisdom and
> revelation as you come to know him, so that, with
> the eyes of your heart enlightened, you may know
> what is the hope to which he has called you.
>
> **—from Ephesians 1:15–23**

When our children were young, dinnertime was always something of a circus. Feats of wonder were performed. For instance, when our son was a toddler, he liked to throw toast over his shoulder, and never once did it land jelly-side up. Adult conversations were often left suspended in midair. See a little girl take the tiniest bite of a vegetable in history! And who needs clown makeup when there is enough spaghetti sauce to go around?

After one long winter weekend, our young family assembled for dinner. It included the usual spirited performances, but I was not amused. Not in the slightest. I was quick to volunteer to clear the table, a precious opportunity for a moment of quiet. When I left, I closed the French doors that separated the dining room from the rest of the house.

As I headed back, I paused, not out of dread, but from something much more compelling. Through the French doors I could see my family. My wife, Karen, was leaning forward, her eyes with a sparkle that was only slightly muted by fatigue. Our son, Todd, was throwing his hands in the air and making indistinguishable noises like a worshiper at a revival meeting. Our daughter, Alanna, was sitting back and giggling, her eyes darting between her mother and her brother.

It was the same rowdy circus, but peering through the panes of the door, I was no longer annoyed. Instead, I felt embraced by the scene. It was something of a revelation. I was able to see my life and those I love with what Paul called "the eyes of the heart enlightened."

Prayer

God, give me enlightened "eyes of the heart," so I might see this world—and you—afresh and so I might have renewed appreciation for the wonder of it all. Amen.

Announcements

And the Word became flesh and lived among us, and
we have seen his glory, the glory as of a parent's
only child, full of grace and truth. . . . From his
fullness we have all received, grace upon grace.

—from John 1:1–18 AUTHOR'S ADAPTATION

It's hard to know where to put the announcements in a worship service. Whether they are placed at the very beginning or before the offering or right before the benediction, announcements can feel like interrupting a prayer with an advertisement. Or, at the very least, it can feel like trying to squeeze in one more person at a beautifully set table. ("Move over, Sermon. I'm so sorry, Anthem. We've got to make room for Announcements.")

Part of the reason announcements don't seem to fit, I think, is that they tend to be all about us, while worship is supposed to be about God. One pastor I know addresses this by insisting there be no godless announcements. That is, if you want to make an announcement, you have to reference God at least once.

Come to think of it, though, worship, properly understood, does not just include announcements—worship itself is one big announcement. It is not an announcement in the way we usually use the term. The center of worship is not announcements of car washes or study groups or trips to the homeless shelter. The center of worship is not about anything we have done or are supposed to do.

Rather, worship is a proclamation of the Good News. It is an announcement of what God has done in Jesus Christ. And this announcement should ring clearly from the beginning to the end of our worship. It turns out that announcement time is the most important of all.

Prayer

God, focus our worship on you and infuse it with praise for all you have done for us. Amen.

Doing a New Thing

*Do not remember the former things, or consider
the things of old. I am about to do a new thing.*
—from Isaiah 43:14–21

It is axiomatic that people often resist change. Lyman Beecher, the great Puritan preacher, was minister of the Congregational church in Litchfield, Connecticut, in the first part of the nineteenth century. During that time, a debate arose in the congregation about whether they would install a woodstove in the meetinghouse. Before then, they had never had any heat at all in the meetinghouse. If it was cold, you would come to worship thickly bundled.

Some in the congregation thought a woodstove would be an improvement, but others were dead set against this new technological intrusion in their sacred space. Eventually, the pro-stove contingent prevailed.

The first Sunday after the stove was installed, some of those who had opposed the installation of the stove complained that the meetinghouse was too hot for them. The men started taking off their jackets and loosening their collars. Some of the women were furiously fanning themselves, trying to stay cool.

Lyman Beecher stood at the pulpit and said, "You will notice that this is the first Sunday we have had our new stove. And next week we will put some wood in it and start a fire."

So, yes, people often resist change. But that is a particularly strange stance for people of faith. After all, we worship a God who declared, "See, I am doing a new thing," the same God who accepts us just as we are but also offers us transformation.

Prayer
God of transformation, do a new thing in my life and in our life together. Amen.

Who Is That Singing?

Philip ran up to [the chariot] and heard him
reading the prophet Isaiah. He asked, "Do you
understand what you are reading?" He replied,
"How can I, unless someone guides me?"

—from Acts 8:26–40

One day, when our children were still very young, a Beatles song came on the radio. I grew up listening to the Beatles so, of course, I began to sing along. Then our daughter, Alanna, asked, "Who is that singing?"

For a moment, I was taken aback by her question. How could she not know who is singing? Isn't that something that is passed on in the genes? And if she doesn't know about the Beatles, what other things have I neglected to tell her?

Obviously, we cannot assume that our children have somehow brought with them, or will pick up somewhere, the most important things we have to share, including the Christian story of God's fierce love for the world.

One does not learn the story by osmosis. It has to be told. After all, the Christian faith is always just one generation away from extinction.

In Acts, we read about an Ethiopian official who, after a visit to Jerusalem, was reading the prophecies of Isaiah while he was riding in a chariot. Philip was inspired to approach the chariot and ask, "Do you understand what you are reading?" And here is the Ethiopian's poignant reply: "How can I, unless someone guides me?"

Exactly. No one is born knowing the story of our faith.

So teach your children, or your grandchildren, or the children of your church the story that has been shared with us. And, somewhere along the line, teach them about the Beatles, too.

Prayer

God, you are here, there, and everywhere. Equip us and inspire us to tell the story that has been shared with us. Amen.

Get Ready to Celebrate

Beware, keep alert; for you do not know when
the time will come. It is like a man going on
a journey, when he leaves home and puts
his slaves in charge, each with his work, and
commands the doorkeeper to be on the watch.
Therefore, keep awake—for you do not know
when the master of the house will come.

—from Mark 13:32–37

In this passage Jesus says that we are to live as if he will return any time. He says that we are to act as if we are servants who do not know the exact moment when the master will come home. So we are to keep alert and be ready, treating each moment as if the master is about to walk through the door.

When I was a teenager and my parents left me on my own while they took a trip out of town, sometimes they would be coy about the time of their return. They wanted to keep me wondering when they would be back so I wouldn't get into mischief while they were away. Is that something like what Jesus is saying here?

Well, perhaps in part. Jesus does expect us to live in an upright manner. But, in the end, preparing for his return also means being ready to celebrate. When our children were young, we always kept party hats and noisemakers in our dining room because we never knew when the events of the day would be cause for celebration.

Birthdays one can prepare for, but other kinds of celebrations require constant preparedness. And when Jesus shows up in big and small ways in our lives, it is cause for great celebration. Will you remember where you have put your party hat and noisemaker? Will you be prepared to whoop it up?

Prayer

Jesus, help me to prepare for your appearance in our world and in my life with a heart that is tuned for joy. Amen.

The Feast in Your Pocket

But he said to them, "You give them
something to eat." They said, "We have no
more than five loaves and two fish."
—from Luke 9:10–17

Jesus is teaching a large crowd until it gets dark. The twelve apostles are hungry and tired at this point. I picture them the way my children used to be on Sunday mornings. Late in the fellowship hour after worship, they would have had enough of church and, tugging on my coat, they would say, "Dad, are we ever going to leave?"

The apostles are something like that. They have had enough of church for a time. They are able to mask their own needs by claiming to have great concern for the people: "This is a remote place and the people look awfully hungry. Shouldn't we send them away so they can get something to eat?"

Jesus responds, "Well, why don't you give them something to eat?" The apostles are dumbfounded: "We only have five loaves and two fish. Look," they say, turning their pockets inside out, "that's it. Unless there is a deli open at this hour, there is no way we are going to be able to feed all these people."

Jesus says, in essence, "Give them what you have. It is enough. Trust that it is enough." And, sure enough, everyone is fed, and there are even plenty of leftovers.

We tend to devalue small things. Jesus never does. Instead, he points to the power in small things that we might so easily overlook. The Realm of God is like a mustard seed, the smallest of all seeds, which grows to be a tree large enough that birds can call it home. The pinch of yeast that leavens the whole loaf. That scrap of bread you brought with you to the hillside that is used to feed five thousand—if you offer it—but only if you offer it.

It starts small. It starts with the feast that is already in your pocket.

Prayer

God, help me to value small things, remembering that the largest of all realities—your Realm—begins with something small. Amen.

Sing One Another's Songs

And with gratitude in your hearts sing psalms,
hymns, and spiritual songs to God.
—from Colossians 3:12–17

In Paul's letter to the Colossians, in the midst of a demanding list of commands to live a righteous life, it is startling to come upon the command to sing: "and with gratitude in your hearts sing psalms, hymns, and spiritual songs to God." Why did they need to be commanded to sing? Isn't singing a great joy?

Well, perhaps the Colossians couldn't agree on what kind of songs to sing. It is amazing how controversial music can be. A while back the Methodists were planning to publish a new hymnal. They started with a survey in which they asked which hymns their members would most like to see included. "Rock of Ages" topped the list. They also asked which hymns they would least like to see included. The number one choice? "Rock of Ages."

It is telling that, in his command to sing, Paul refers to three different kinds of music: "psalms" (that is, songs from the Bible), "hymns" (songs of praise not from the Bible), and "spiritual songs," which could mean just about anything. Sing psalms, hymns, *and* spiritual songs. So Paul was saying, "Sing different songs. Even in a style you don't like, because it may be speaking from the heart, or to the heart, of someone else in your community of faith."

That may be why Paul had to command the people of Colossae to sing. To sing together—songs from our different cultures, languages, backgrounds, and, yes, musical tastes—can be a radical act. It would be wonderful if it could be said of our congregations: "It is the kind of place where they joyfully sing one another's songs."

Prayer

God, tune my heart for praise so that I might sing joyfully and, in singing, be drawn together with all who worship you. Amen.

The Things That Last

> As he came out of the temple, one of his
> disciples said to him, "Look, Teacher, what
> large stones and what large buildings!"
> —from Mark 13:1–2

In New York City you can always spot the visitors. It's not from the way they are dressed, because you can dress any way you like in New York. It isn't from their accents, because New Yorkers may have grown up in Kansas City or Katmandu. Rather, the telltale sign of visitors is that they are always looking up, trying to take in the tops of the buildings.

That is how I picture the disciples as they entered Jerusalem with Jesus: "Look, Teacher, what large stones and what large buildings!"

Jesus responded, "There will not be one stone left upon another," putting the Temple, in all its magnificence, into a different perspective. Like all human achievements, it was little more than a sandcastle that was destined to be swept away.

We are forever confusing the lasting and the momentary. When Jesus was brought before the chief priests, he was accused of saying, "I will destroy this Temple that is made with hands and in three days I will build another, not made with hands." The priests were incensed: Surely no one can destroy the Temple. It will stand forever. And what is this nonsense about building a temple in three days? Any temple that could be built in three days would be felled by the first brisk wind.

But, sure enough, the Temple that the priests and disciples admired no longer stands. And there *was* a temple built within three days of Jesus's death, and it is still standing—the church, a never-ending testament to the ever-living Christ.

Prayer

Jesus, help me not to confuse the lasting and the momentary so that I might follow you more faithfully. Amen.

Mystery in the Sand

The heavens are telling the glory of God.
—from Psalm 19

There is a beautiful secluded beach that, unbelievably, is only about fifty miles from Manhattan, as the crow flies (a funny expression, now that I think of it, because there are no crows here, only the occasional seagull). I have walked on this beach countless times because I have gone there since I was a boy.

In many ways my walk this day was idyllic. The sun, which had been brutal earlier in the day, was taking a final bow over the dunes. The waves seemed to be relaxing a bit after a long day of continuous exercise. And, yes, since this is a true story (all my stories are true), I should also add there were black flies biting at my ankles almost the whole time.

Then I encountered something of a mystery. Every so often there were little arrows written in the sand, sometimes a whole series of them. Some pointed to the sunset over the dunes. Others seemed to be calling my attention to the surf. Obviously, someone was bidding me to pay attention, eager for me not to miss the grandeur of the scene. I looked up and down the beach to see if I could figure out who had left these markers, but there was no one for hundreds of yards in either direction.

I continued to ponder the mystery until I came across a seagull, who walked toward the water when she saw me coming and—you guessed it—she left little trident arrows in the sand as she walked, calling me to attention.

I thought, "The heavens are telling the glory of God. And so are the seagulls."

Prayer
God, if it is true that prayer is paying attention, call me to attention in any way you choose. Amen.

Rationalize or Confess?

Happy are those whose transgression is forgiven.
—from Psalm 32

I used to say that if I were to start my own business, it would be called We Can Rationalize Anything. Just bring something you have done or anticipate doing, and I will help you rationalize it. Of course, it wasn't long before I realized that this business would be a complete bust. Although there is great demand for rationalizations, most people know very well how to come up with their own.

The alternative to rationalization is confession. Some people tell me they don't like prayers of confession in worship. When they talk about their experience of confession, it sounds about as appealing as a trip to the vice principal's office. But confession, when it is followed by an assurance of pardon, can be something quite different—more like being shown the way to freedom after a time of captivity.

After all, there is something wonderfully freeing about facing the truth about ourselves. Some people may need to believe that they are lovable, but Christians are free to recognize that we are not always lovable, because we know that God loves us anyway. The point of confession is not to feel bad about ourselves, but rather to cling to the goodness of God.

There was a self-help book a while back titled *I'm Okay, You're Okay*. William Sloane Coffin liked to point out that the Christian version of that affirmation is more like *I'm Not Okay, You're Not Okay, but That's Okay*. Coffin's version is an assurance of God's forgiveness. That's why I don't think of confession as anything like a trip to the vice principal's office.

Prayer
God, although I sometimes shrink from confession, help me to be open with you. I will cling to your goodness. Amen.

A Father-in-Law's Love

Jethro said, "Blessed be the Lord, who
has delivered you from the Egyptians
and from Pharaoh. Now I know that the
Lord is greater than all gods, because he
delivered the people from the Egyptians."
—Exodus 18:10–11

The love most parents have for their children comes naturally. It is not worthy of much praise. Indeed, it is expected that parents will love their own children. After all, parents are genetically predisposed to love their children.

This is not the case with parents-in-law. There is nothing natural about the love of parents-in-law and, in fact, in-law relationships can be notoriously challenging. And so, parents-in-law are frequently the butt of jokes.

Because love is not expected from a parent-in-law in the same way it is expected from a parent, the love of a parent-in-law can be particularly touching in its generosity. Such was the love of Jethro for Moses.

Jethro had to be one of the best fathers-in-law ever. When Moses killed a man in Egypt and fled to the foreign land of Midian, Jethro took him in and even "gave" Moses his daughter Zipporah to marry. Then Jethro gave Moses a job in his fields, where Moses stayed for forty years. When Moses was convinced that he needed to go to Egypt to lead the people of Israel out of Egypt, Jethro took in Zipporah and her two sons and cared for them while Moses was away.

Then, when Moses finally returned to Jethro's household after the Exodus, Jethro blessed Moses and his God. Jethro's support is all the more remarkable because he was neither a Jew nor an Egyptian, so he had nothing at stake personally in these larger events. But he loved Moses.

The love of this father-in-law was no joke. It was a generous love worthy of praise and emulation.

Prayer

Thank you, God, for those who extend to me a generous love that is beyond expectation. Amen.

Before You Eat That Carrot . . .

While they were eating, he took a
loaf of bread, and after blessing it
he broke it [and] gave it to them.
—Mark 14:22

Researchers have found that performing a simple ritual before a meal can enhance the experience—the flavor of the food is intensified; the meal is enjoyed more. I knew this even before reading the research. After all, I enjoy wolfing down a brownie left in the pan, but that experience doesn't compare to the way I will savor a piece of birthday cake after the ritual of singing and blowing out candles.

In one experiment, students were instructed to perform a ritual before eating a carrot: Knock twice on the table before grabbing a bag of carrots, then knock twice more, take a deep breath, and then eat a carrot. Consistently the researchers found that the knocking-breathing ritual enhanced the students' enjoyment of the carrot.

It is interesting that watching a ritual—such as watching a waiter open a bottle of wine—does not have the same effect. Only a ritual you perform yourself can do that.

The researchers defined rituals as "a series of behaviors that are seemingly irrelevant to the act that follows."

Well, not all rituals performed before meals are "irrelevant to the act that follows"—for instance, the ritual of offering "grace" or "thanks" before a meal. Such a ritual is a fitting expression of gratitude for the gifts of the table. That it may enhance our experience is a bonus.

So knock on the table, if you must. Take a deep breath while you're at it. Then offer a prayer, such as this one (which can be sung to the tune of the Doxology):

Praise God from whom all blessings flow,
Praise God all creatures here below,
Praise God for all that love has done,
Creator, Christ, and Spirit one. Amen.

On Feeling Small

When I look at your heavens, the work of your fingers, the moon and the stars that you have established, what are human beings that you are mindful of them, mortals that you care for them?

—Psalm 8:3–4

When I spend time at the ocean, I can feel very small. The horizon is so distant that it is nothing except the limit of human sight. Sometimes the waves are so powerful that they can toss a grown man about like a fragile toy. At night the sky is sequined with stars that are beyond counting.

Even picking up a handful of sand can be awe-inspiring if you remember the oft-cited comparison that there are as many stars in the universe as there are grains of sand on the earth. Of course, no one really knows how many stars or grains of sand there are, but the point remains—there are a whole lot of both.

There is value in being brought down to size every once in a while. After all, most of us live with an inflated sense of self-importance. We can become as puffed up as one of those balloons in the Macy's Thanksgiving Day Parade.

So it is good to be reminded just how small we are. But that doesn't mean it is easy. Oftentimes, to feel small is to feel vulnerable, insignificant, perhaps even of no account.

That is one reason why, when I have spent time by the ocean, I am particularly eager to get to worship. There, I still feel small in the presence of our awesome God, but I am also reminded that God values small things—mustard seeds, pinches of yeast, sparrows—most of all.

Prayer

God, when I experience your magnificence, I can feel very small, so I am grateful for the assurance that you love small things. Amen.

Be Quick about It

You must understand this, my beloved: let everyone
be quick to listen, slow to speak, slow to anger.
—from James 1:17–27

James reminds us that there are some things we should be quick to do, like listen, and other things we should be slow to do, like talk and express anger.

We might want to expand the lists. Here are some things I want to be slow to do: presume that I really understand what is going on in another person's life; be convinced that I am right; walk away from a friendship; assume that someone meant to hurt me; say something that may wound another; conclude there is nothing I can do to help; think that what someone else most needs is my advice. It's not that it is always inappropriate to do any of these things, but oftentimes it is, which is reason enough to slow down and reflect.

And here are some things that I want to be quick to do: express appreciation; extend forgiveness; offer encouragement; apologize when I know I have messed up; stand up for the oppressed; offer words of confession; remember the promises of God; praise God in all circumstances; keep quiet when I cannot improve upon the silence. All these things may sound good in the abstract, but the point is to do them now and not delay.

As philosopher Henri-Frédéric Amiel affirmed, "Life is short, and there is little time to gladden the hearts of those who journey with us . . . so be quick to love and make haste to be kind."

Prayer
O God, help me to be slow to do those things that may do harm
and quick to do those things that I should do right now. Amen.

God Does Not Like Whiners

Why have you brought us up out of Egypt,
to bring us to this wretched place?

—from Numbers 20:1–13

One of the messages from this passage in the book of Numbers is easily summarized: God does not like whiners. God had just led the people of Israel out of slavery in Egypt when they started whining about where they ended up, in a land where there was little vegetation and no visible source of water. In response, God told Moses to strike a rock and water poured out of it. But God was not too happy with the kvetching Israelites and said, in essence, "This group of whiners is never going to make it to the Promised Land."

God doesn't always expect us to be cheery. In fact, it is evident from scripture that God welcomes lament and even complaint as legitimate responses to the hardships of life. The difference is that whiners always find a way to whine, regardless of their circumstances.

They tell a story in Vermont about a farmer who always bemoaned his crop yields. Every harvest seemed to fall short. Then, one year, after a spectacular bumper crop, a fellow farmer said, "Well, even you will have to admit that this was a good year." To which the whining farmer replied, "Yes, but terribly hard on the soil."

Whiners always find reason to whine. And those whose lives are marked by gratitude always find reason to give thanks. It is clear which kind of person God expects us to be.

Prayer

God, please hear my complaints when life is difficult, but, dear God, please don't let me become a whiner. Instead, animate my heart with gratitude. Amen.

Name Change

But Saul, also known as Paul, filled with the
Holy Spirit, looked intently at him.
—from Acts 13:1–12

Names are important. A name is so much more than, say, a label attached to a jar. We identify with our names. For instance, I feel so closely identified with my name that if I had a different name, I feel as if I would be a different person. And when we change our name, it usually marks a big change in our life.

When our daughter, Alanna, was very young, she could not pronounce her name, so she called herself "Lala"; we did, too. Then one day when I called her Lala, she announced, "I am not Lala. I am Alanna." In that statement she was not only pronouncing her name, she was also announcing that she was now a big girl. No one ever called her Lala again.

Saul had been a persecutor of Christians. When he had his own encounter with the risen Christ, however, his life was changed forever. He too became a follower of the Way—just like those he had formerly persecuted. The change was so dramatic and so complete that his old name simply no longer fit. This new person needed a new name. So he became known as Paul.

And when you or I are baptized, we are given a new name, the name of Jesus Christ (in fact, some people speak of baptism as "christening"—literally, taking on the name of Christ). In baptism his name is now part of your name. How might that realization change the way you approach the day?

Prayer

O God, you call each of us by name, but you also give us a new name, the name of Jesus Christ. Help me to live into—and up to—the implications of that name change. Amen.

Introverts
and Extroverts

If the whole body were an eye,
where would the hearing be? If the
whole body were hearing, where
would the sense of smell be?

—from 1 Corinthians 12:14–26

I am convinced Jesus was an introvert. After all, he was a pastor who was always running away from his congregation. His ministry was characterized by intense engagement with people in rhythm with time alone or with a few close friends.

By contrast, clearly the garrulous Paul was an extrovert. Some of his letters have the quality of someone thinking out loud, a telltale characteristic of an extrovert (see, for instance, 2 Corinthians 11). We can imagine Paul spending time alone only when he was thrown in jail, and even then, he would be attempting to convert the person in the next cell with the incessancy of an extrovert.

The generative pairing of Jesus and Paul reminds us that introverts and extroverts can collaborate fruitfully, and it might even be said that we need each other.

A congregation benefits from having both introverts and extroverts, particularly if they understand each other—or, at least, understand enough to keep from driving each other nuts. The different clusters of character traits associated with introverts and extroverts are not to be moderated but drawn upon, much as spiritual gifts are, for the betterment of the community. If Paul were aware of the typology, he might have reminded the Corinthians, "If all were extroverts, where would the practice of careful listening be? If all were introverts, who would greet the newcomers at the fellowship hour?"

Prayer

God, since no single person can be all things and evidence all gifts, thank you for bundling us together in community so that we can benefit from the gifts of others. Amen.

Thou Art with Me

I will fear no evil, for thou art with me.
—from Psalm 23 KJV

Every parent knows what it is like to be awakened in the middle of the night by the cries of a child who has had a nightmare. Sometimes the fears are easily quelled: "Daddy, I think there are bears in my closet." "No, there are no bears." "How do you know?" "I'll turn on the light and you'll see."

Other times, however, the fears expressed are not those confined to childhood: "Mommy, I'm afraid of being alone." "Daddy, does *everyone* die?" We stumble through our responses. On such occasions, we become painfully aware of the limits of words. We are relieved when the child says, "Just stay with me"; relieved to learn that the child is not looking for magic words, but for the gift of presence. We are able to respond easily: "Yes, yes, of course I will stay with you."

But then there is one more question: "Will you stay with me no matter what?" Then it is your turn to sense the stir of fear and to feel tears appear in your own eyes because you know that, although you can stay with the child tonight and, if need be, for many nights in the future, there will come a time, perhaps a night much darker than the child has ever experienced, when she will cry out and you will not be there.

This psalm, with its assurance of God's continued presence no matter what a day may hold, was written for that parent and that child: "I will fear no evil, for thou art with me."

Prayer
God, I am so grateful that there is no road I might take that I must travel alone. Amen.

Do You Have Anything to Eat?

> While in their joy they were disbelieving
> and still wondering, he said to them,
> "Have you anything here to eat?"
>
> —from Luke 24:36–49

Jesus asks a lot of questions in the Gospels—307, to be exact. Even when the risen Christ appears to the disciples, he is still asking questions. We might assume that, on this occasion at least, he would have settled for declarative sentences. And if he were to ask questions at such a time, we would expect those questions to be momentous ones. But one question he asks seems anything but momentous. According to Luke, soon after Jesus appeared to his disciples, he asks, "Do you have anything here to eat?"

What do you make of that? That doesn't sound like the question of a risen Lord. It sounds more like the question of a teenager arriving home from school.

So his disciples give Jesus a piece of broiled fish and he eats it.

Apparently, rising from the dead really works up an appetite. Who knew? Get this fellow something to eat!

What's going on here? Well, for one, it's a way for Luke to affirm that Jesus's presence is real. He isn't a ghost.

But, knowing Jesus, the follow-up question is this: "Does your neighbor have anything to eat?" After all, this is the same Jesus who taught us to pray, "Give us this day our daily bread." Not *my* daily bread, *our* daily bread. It is a collective plea, not an individual one. In this prayer that we say so often is the radical notion that your neighbor's need is not different from your own need. There is only *our* need.

Fifteen centuries ago, Saint Benedict wrote that Jesus comes to us disguised in every stranger knocking on the door asking for hospitality and asking for food. And if that is true, the question on his lips surely is: "Do you have anything here to eat?"

That turns out to be a momentous question.

Prayer

Jesus, give me eyes to see you, especially in your distressing disguise as one of the poor. Amen.

We Need More Saints

Time would fail me to tell of Gideon, Barak, Samson,
Jephthah, of David and Samuel and the prophets—
who through faith conquered kingdoms, administered
justice, obtained promises, shut the mouths of
lions, quenched raging fire, escaped the edge of
the sword, won strength out of weakness, became
mighty in war, put foreign armies to flight.

—from Hebrews 11:29–38

We Protestants need more saints. In this context, I do not mean *saint* in the way the apostle Paul used the term as inclusive of all the people of God. Rather, I am referring to individuals of faith whom the church points to and says, in essence, "Pay attention to these lives. Take inspiration from them. Try, as you are able, to follow their example." I am thinking of Frederick Buechner's definition: "In God's holy flirtation with the world, God occasionally drops a handkerchief. These handkerchiefs are called saints."

Sometimes, when I listen to Protestant preachers (which, of course, includes me), it can seem as if we have concluded there are only a small handful of people whose lives reflect God's glory. The Roman Catholics have over ten thousand canonized saints. By my count, we Protestants have as few as five: Óscar Romero, Martin Luther King Jr., Mother Teresa, Nelson Mandela, Dietrich Bonhoeffer. Of course, these individuals are great examples of faith. They are saints, to be sure. But when their names are invoked so often, and other examples drawn upon so seldom, it does not help us envision the range of ways one's life can reflect God.

So I envy the Roman Catholics their saints because they have many people of history to whom they can point. To be sure, some of them are rather quirky (like Saint Neot, who did his daily devotions while neck deep in a well and, thus, became the patron saint of fish) and others whose qualifications for sainthood seem rather thin (like Simeon of Stylites, whose chief accomplishment seems to have been sitting on a pillar for decades at a time). But the sheer variety of saints in the Roman Catholic tradition stretches the imagination to encompass the multitude of ways a human life can manifest the Holy Spirit.

Who are some of the saints you have encountered recently?

Prayer

God, give us more saints. We need all the inspiration and instruction we can get. Amen.

Planting Unlikely Seeds

I planted, Apollos watered,
but God gave the growth.
—from 1 Corinthians 3:5–9

When I was in high school, I taught a Sunday school class of fifth-grade boys. I was not a very good teacher. And I am not being falsely modest here. Winston Churchill said about one of his contemporaries: "He is a modest man who has much to be modest about." As a teacher, I had much to be modest about.

Saturday night was usually a late night for me. I wouldn't look at the Sunday school curriculum until Sunday morning, and then with bleary eyes. That's about as far as the lesson planning went. I didn't know how to make the material interesting. The boys in the class were bored and were not beyond telling me so. And a large group of bored fifth-grade boys is not a pretty sight. So, much of the time, I felt like I was running out the clock. When each week's class finally ended, the boys would run out the door as if freed from prison.

Imagine my surprise some twenty years later, when I got this phone call: "Hello, Martin? This is Justin Peterson. You were my fifth-grade Sunday school teacher. I've thought back on that class so many times."

Uh-oh. I couldn't imagine where this conversation was headed. "I've become active in the Presbyterian church in our town. They asked me to be a deacon. And I think it all started in that Sunday school class you taught." Really? "Anyway, I'm getting married this summer and I would be honored if you would perform the ceremony."

It was one of the most surprising conversations I have ever had. I still don't think I was any good as a Sunday school teacher. But somehow a seed was planted, and then it was watered, and God gave it growth. You just never know.

Prayer

God, help me to plant seeds with joyful abandon because only you know where they will take root. Amen.

One Person at a Time

Are not five sparrows sold for
two pennies? Yet not one of them
is forgotten in God's sight.

—from Luke 12:4–7

Saint Augustine said that God is able to love each person as if he or she were the only person in the world. But we cannot do that. As human beings, we are limited in that way. Sometimes, however, we can love one particular person in that intensely focused way. It could be a spouse, or a partner, or a friend. And to love one person that completely is to catch a glimpse of how much God cares for each one of us.

In the movie *Shall We Dance?*, the character played by Susan Sarandon reflects on why people get married: "We need a witness to our lives. There's a billion people on the planet. I mean, what does any one life mean? But in a marriage, you're promising to care about everything. The good things, the bad things, the terrible things, the mundane things . . . all of it, all of the time, every day. You're saying, 'Your life will not go unnoticed, because I will notice it. Your life will not go unwitnessed, because I will be your witness.'"

What that character said about marriage also can be said of close and abiding friendships. Our love may not be able to encompass everyone—at least not fully. But sometimes we can love one person as if he or she were the only person in the world. We can promise to care about everything. We can bear witness to that person's life. At the heart of the Christian gospel is the affirmation that God in Christ is the witness to our lives, all of our lives. It is a love of which we can catch glimpses in our relationships with one another, one person at a time.

Prayer

God, help me today to bear witness faithfully to the lives of those I love—and, in so doing, may I catch a glimpse of the ways you love everyone. Amen.

I'll Just Say "Amen" to That

> Let no evil talk come out of your mouths, but only
> what is useful for building up, as there is need, so
> that your words may give grace to those who hear.
> —Ephesians 4:29

Early in my ministry, I served First Congregational Church in Burlington, Vermont, with Thelma Norton, the longtime parish visitor. She was almost three times my age when I came to the church. In my nine years there, she taught me a great deal by her example. For instance, she would never utter a word of complaint about a parishioner. If she began to approach doing anything like that, she would stop herself—sometimes in mid-sentence—and say, "Well, I'll just say 'Amen' to that." Then she would change the subject.

When I was serving another church a number of decades later, members of the church leadership were wrestling with some complaints from a few particularly grumpy parishioners. That made us rather grumpy ourselves. We even started to complain about the complainers. Somewhere in that conversation I reminded myself and my colleagues about Thelma's catchphrase. We were able to move on. The next week someone brought to the meeting bright yellow cards with the words "Well, I'll just say 'Amen' to that" printed on them. Without any coordination, we all posted those cards in our offices, just in case we needed the reminder—which of course we did on a regular basis.

It is much the same reminder offered to the Ephesians: "Let no evil talk come out of your mouths, but only what is useful for building up." It is so simple: Say those things that build up. Don't say those things that tear down. It is said that in successful marriages, two or three things are left unsaid each day. And it is true of other relationships as well. Thank you, Thelma.

Prayer

O God, help me to hold my tongue when I am about to tear someone down. And when I need to be critical of another, may it only be in ways that, in the end, build up. Amen to that.

An Offering You Can't Refuse

> He looked up and saw rich people putting their gifts
> into the treasury; he also saw a poor widow put in
> two small copper coins. He said, "Truly I tell you, this
> poor widow has put in more than all of them; for all of
> them have contributed out of their abundance, but she
> out of her poverty has put in all she had to live on."
>
> —Luke 21:1–4

I have a recurring dream. Someone calls me on the phone and invites me to lunch. Over lunch that person says, "Martin, I am aware that the church is pressed for funds, particularly in this financial climate, and the church has to spend so much energy to raise those funds. Well, I came into some money this year, so I want to cover this year's entire church budget with my own gift."

First, I try to catch my breath. Then I offer to pay for lunch. But the person goes on: "I ask only one thing,"

I say, "Sure. Whatever. Would you like some champagne?"

"No, thank you," he says. "All I ask is that you not accept any other contributions or offerings for the rest of the year. I want to do it all. My gift to the congregation."

Then I take another deep breath and say, "I'm sorry, but I cannot accept your gift. I can't do that to the people. It's not just a matter of being able to pay the bills. We need to be able to respond to all that God is doing in our midst and to share in that work. We can't be deprived of the opportunity to give of ourselves. To hear the promises of God and to receive the gifts of God, and to be unable to respond? Why, that's a burden. We just can't do that to the people."

A contribution and an offering are different: We make a contribution because the church needs money. We make an offering because we need to give. Only some are able to give a large contribution. Anyone is able to make a great offering.

Prayer

Giver of every good and perfect gift, accept this gift of mine, that I might share in your work and that your work might prosper. Amen.

The Familiar Stranger

The father said to his slaves, "... Get the fatted calf and kill it, and let us eat and celebrate; for this son of mine was dead and is alive again; he was lost and is found!"

—from Luke 15:11–32

Two old friends meet in the park. Upon seeing each other, they don't say a word. They sit on a park bench in silence for the longest time. Then one finally breaks the silence by saying, "Oy." The other responds, "Oy." To which the first replies, "Well, enough about the children." We may not know the details, but we know this: Family relationships are perhaps the most challenging of all.

A mother once told me about how she struggles to understand her son and wondered aloud how a single gene pool could produce two people who are so different from one another. She said, "In some ways, it's like living with a stranger." Her comment is a reminder that sometimes the strangers who need our hospitality do not come from a foreign land. They may be as close as across the breakfast table. And, of course, it is from the word *stranger* that we get the word *estranged*. The member of your family with whom you are estranged is someone who has become a stranger to you.

Is there someone in your life, perhaps very close, perhaps even a member of your own family, who is like a stranger to you? Rather than feeling ashamed that a relationship that was meant to be close has come to that, perhaps it is better just to treat that person like a stranger. And in our tradition we are called upon to receive the stranger, to create a safe place for the stranger. In the practice of hospitality, the stranger has a special role to play. It is by making room for the stranger—perhaps a very familiar stranger—that we make room for God.

So let me ask again: Is there someone in your life, perhaps even a member of your own family, who is like a stranger to you? Well, go ahead, treat him, treat her, like a stranger.

Prayer

Come, Holy Spirit, come, and give me the gift of hospitality to strangers, even familiar ones. Amen.

All Have Sinned.
I'll Drink to That!

All have sinned and fall short of the glory of God.
—from Romans 3:21–26 NIV

Perhaps you saw the movie *Patton*, which won the Academy Award for best film in 1970. In that movie, George C. Scott gave a memorable performance as the controversial American World War II general George S. Patton.

One scene was particularly memorable. The war is over and General Patton is having dinner with some Russian generals. Patton never trusted the Russians. He doesn't want to sit at the table with them. That is clear from his every word and gesture.

After dinner, the ranking Russian general offers a conciliatory toast. When he is finished, Patton stands and says to the translator, with a smile, "Thank the general, and tell him that I have no desire to drink with him or any other Russian son of a bitch." The shocked translator turns ashen. Patton gestures to him in a way that says, "Go on, do as I say."

Patton and the Russian general continue to smile at each other as the translator begins to convey Patton's message. Their smiles are still frozen on their faces when the Russian general offers his response to Patton. The translator then turns to Patton: "He says he thinks you are a son of a bitch, too." After a pause, Patton lifts his glass and says, "All right, tell him I'll drink to that!" And they drink together.

We may not use that kind of language in church, but we cannot deny that we are all flawed and faulty creatures. "All have sinned and fall short of the glory of God" is the way the apostle Paul put it. And that is one of the bases of our community as Christians. We recognize that we are all sinners. We all stand in need of forgiveness.

All of us are invited to join the party and sit at the table together—not on the basis of what we have done, but on the basis of what God has done for all of us.

Prayer

Thank you for calling us into a community of imperfect people who are loved perfectly by you. Amen.

From *My* to *Our*

Give us this day our daily bread.
—from Matthew 6:9–15

Researchers at the University of Pennsylvania have been studying our use of pronouns in Facebook posts. They discovered that the use of first-person singular pronouns like *I* and *me* is higher among younger users. Older folks tend to use more first-person plural pronouns, like *we* and *our*.

James Pennebaker, a social scientist, offers a reason for the discrepancy: "When we are in new situations and are trying to establish an identity, we tend to be more self-focused, which comes out through higher rates of *I* words."

Of course, not all young people are self-focused, and not all older people are focused on others. Nevertheless, a mark of maturity—at whatever age—is the movement from more *I* and *me* language to more *we* and *our* language.

So when someone starts on a spiritual path, we can expect references to "my spirituality" or "my faith journey." It is language of being new and starting out. But if one remains devoted to the trinity of "me, myself, and I," eventually it is no longer appropriate. Spiritual maturity comes with being able to use the language of community, including the pronouns *we*, *our*, and *us*.

And so Jesus prays, "Give *us* this day *our* daily bread." Who is this *us* to which Jesus refers? Not just his family or his small circle of friends. And Jesus isn't merely referring to his followers, either. His is a very big *us*—the biggest *us* possible, actually. It encompasses the largest community of all—the whole human family.

Prayer
God, help me to move—each day—from an *I* and *me* approach to life to the spirit of *us* and *our* reflected in Jesus's prayer. Amen.

Forgiving and Forgetting

I will forgive their iniquity, and
remember their sin no more.

—Jeremiah 31:34

In my experience, when someone says, "I will forgive, but I will never forget," I always wonder if they are truly ready to forgive. Forgiveness requires something that is not forgetfulness in the strict sense, but that is akin to forgetfulness.

In his masterpiece *City of God*, Saint Augustine says that when we are redeemed in the world to come, we will still remember our own wrongdoing clearly enough, but we will no longer remember the pain associated with our wrongdoing.

In the book of Jeremiah, the prophet announces God's new covenant and makes a promise: "I will forgive their iniquity and remember their sins no more." In forgiving, God chooses not to remember.

We are not expected to erase every memory of hurt or injustice from our cerebral "hard drives." Rather, we are to forgive so completely that it is as if we have forgotten.

The Danish philosopher Søren Kierkegaard put it this way: Choosing to forget hurt or injustice suffered at the hands of another is like taking something and putting it behind your back—it's still there and, if you are asked about it, you would have to grant that it exists. But you don't look at it. It's not between you, but rather behind you. He writes, "The one who loves forgives in this way: in love he turns toward the one he forgives; but when he turns toward him, he of course cannot see what is lying behind his back."

Clara Barton, the founder of the American Red Cross, was famous for her generous temperament. She never bore grudges. Once she was reminded by a friend of a wrong done to her some years earlier. "Don't you remember?" asked her friend. "No," replied Clara firmly. "I distinctly remember forgetting that." In other words, she had put it behind her.

Prayer

God, forgive him (or her), because I find it difficult to forgive. And then help me to share that point of view, that blessed forgetfulness in which what was between us is now behind me. Amen.

Breathing Spaces

Jesus said to them again, "Peace be with you. As the Father
has sent me, so I send you." When he had said this, he
breathed on them and said to them, "Receive the Holy Spirit."
—John 20:21–22

In our already overcrowded lives, another space is being taken
away.

When I was learning to write, I was taught that you should
have two spaces after a period before starting a new sentence.
Now we are told, by no less an arbiter than *The Chicago Manual
of Style*, that one space is the norm.

The primary reason the *Chicago* authors cite for preferring
a single space is efficiency. Of course, it all comes down to efficiency, as so much seems to these days. They conclude that
typing two spaces "is inefficient, requiring an extra keystroke
for every sentence." An extra keystroke? Well, that is simply too
much to ask, don't you think?

But I think we need to be fighting for more space, not less.
Space gives us breathing room, which is another way of saying
that space allows for the inspiration of the Holy Spirit.

J. R. R. Tolkien told the story of correcting student essays,
when he came upon a blank page among the papers. He stared at
it for a moment and then wrote upon it, "In a hole in the ground
there lived a hobbit." It just came to him like a revelation. And
that's how he started his book *The Hobbit*, the novel that leads
into *The Lord of the Rings* trilogy. But for that inspiration, he
needed that blank page, just a little space between all those words.

Just a little space. The Holy Spirit can work with that.

Prayer
Dear God, today I offer a silent prayer, just a little breathing
room, a little space for you to write upon my heart. Amen.

Finding Ourselves in the Lost and Found

Which one of you, having a hundred sheep and losing one
of them, does not leave the ninety-nine in the wilderness
and go after the one that is lost until he finds it?

—from Luke 15:3–7

In Jesus's parable, the shepherd leaves ninety-nine sheep to save the one that is lost. When he finds the lost sheep, he is so tipsy with joy that he throws a party. And at this party the sheep is not the main dish; he's the guest of honor.

If you are one of the ninety-nine who were left in the fold, that is not a very satisfying end to the story. You might feel ignored, deserted even. Why is attention lavished on the one who is in need and so little attention given to the others? Is that fair? If you are one of the ninety-nine, it may not seem so.

But our lives are such that we all are lost sometime.

We are forever encountering fresh examples of this: the once vigorous man who now cannot walk across the room without assistance; the woman who now has to be introduced to her daughter every time they visit; the self-made man whose business is now in a shambles; the woman who returned home to find her partner packing his bags.

You see, there really are no ninety-nine forever safely tucked into the fold. We all get to be lost sometime.

A mother of eight children was asked if she had any favorites. She replied, "Favorites? Yes, I have favorites. I love the one who is sickest until he is well. I love the one who is in trouble until she is safe again. And I love the one who is farthest away until he comes home."

That is the Good News: God has a special attachment to those who are lost. And we all get to be lost sometime.

Prayer

God, please stay with me when I am in the safety of the fold, and seek me out when I am one of the lost. Amen.

May I Remind You?

But now, dear lady, I ask you, not as
though I were writing you a new
commandment, but one we have had from
the beginning, let us love one another.
—from 2 John 1–6

In this harried age, when we want to catch the latest news and we eagerly devour information, it is easy to underestimate the power of reminders. In our vocabulary, "I've already heard that" usually translates to "You didn't need to tell me."

But reminders are important. I think of the Vermont couple celebrating their fortieth wedding anniversary. Vermonters are not known for expressing their emotions freely, but on this occasion the wife turns to her husband and says, "You know, Harold, you never tell me you love me." He replies, "Well, I told you that when I married you. If anything changes, I'll let you know."

And yet sometimes we need to hear something we have heard many times before.

I have a friend who says that he goes to worship to be reminded of what he believes. The Good News is also an old, old story. It is the story of God's passionate love affair with the world. We've heard it all before, but we can no more tire of this story than we can tire of the words *I love you*, which, of course, is just the message that this story brings—God's love made known to us.

So John does not write a newsy letter to his "dear lady." Instead, he is content with offering an important reminder of a commandment they had heard many times before: "Let us love one another."

Sometimes the Good News is in the form of a good reminder.

Prayer

O God of the evening news and the Good News, create in me the space and the inclination to receive reminders of your love and your commandment that we love one another. Amen.

Finding God in
All the Wrong Places

[God] has made [Christ] the head over all
things for the church, which is his body,
the fullness of him who fills all in all.

—Ephesians 1:22–23

On a number of occasions, I have hiked in the interior reaches of the Grand Canyon. To me it is a holy place, the most vaulted of natural gothic cathedrals. It's not hard to feel close to God there, not only because of what is present, but also due to what is largely absent—the demands of living in community. The buttes don't quarrel with each other. The California condors make no demands of the living. The rollicking streams offer only comforting words. There is no need to raise money for a sanctuary roof, because the blue sky has already supplied it. In such a place, I relate easily to those who testify that their surest encounters with God are in the natural world.

Nevertheless, the affirmation that God can be found most easily outside the church has never seemed like much of a claim. The true wonder is that God can be found inside the church, among quirky, flawed, and broken people who may have little in common and yet are bound to one another. What an unlikely setting in which to encounter God. But the Christian God seems to like to surprise us by showing up in the most unpromising places, like a Jew from Nazareth and in a motley gathering of people known as the church.

God throws us together in the church and says, in essence, "Here is where you get a chance to learn how to live with other people, to forgive, and even come to see God in one another. After all, if you can find God here, you can find God anywhere."

The church, like the family, is the place where we learn to live with people we are stuck with. And when we stick with those we are stuck with, it is a living reminder of the God who is stuck with us all.

Prayer

God, give me eyes to see you at work, particularly in surprising places. Amen.

A Funeral for a Frog

O death, where is your victory?
O death, where is your sting?

—1 Corinthians 15:55 NASB

"Shady is dead," my wife, Karen, said to me, with more concern than grief in her voice. I knew the source of her concern well enough. Shady had lived in a tank in our den for a year and a half, as close to family as a frog can be.

How do we break the news to our daughter, Alanna, just five years old at the time, who referred to herself as the frog's "master," who gave Shady her name, and even informed us that Shady was a girl ("because there's some way to tell," she had said)?

When Alanna woke up, I told her, "I have some sad news. Shady died." Alanna immediately responded, "How can you tell?" I had to suppress a smile because, in truth, the frog was the picture of death, lying belly-up with her webbed "hands" positioned as if to hold a lily. I said, "Come downstairs and see."

Alanna stared at Shady for a long time and said, "She's dead," then added matter-of-factly, "We should have a funeral."

Alanna knew the very spot to bury her. When the hole was deep enough, I slid Shady's body into the ground and we covered her with a blanket of earth.

"Let's sing a song," Alanna said. I asked if she had any suggestions. "Let's sing 'Silent Night.'" With the rain beginning to fall around us, seeming to water the seed we had planted in the earth, we sang a homely duet. Then Alanna said a prayer: "Dear God, thank you for Shady, who was a great frog. We hope she is all right. Please take care of her. Amen." We placed a couple of evergreen boughs on the grave and then went inside for breakfast.

I suppose it is handy to have a minister in the family when a frog needs a funeral, but in this case I was more member of the congregation than officiant. And I was struck by how wonderful it is to be part of a family, the church, that shows us from the earliest age how to respond to the awesome presence of death.

Prayer

Thank you for comfort in the presence of death. And thank you, again, for Shady and all the small creatures who have graced our lives. Amen.

The Shape of a Table

Beware of the scribes, who like to walk around
in long robes . . . and to have the best seats in the
synagogues and places of honor at banquets.

—Luke 20:46

The shape of the tables around which we gather is significant. Anyone who is old enough to remember the Vietnam War, as I am, will remember how the first weeks and months of the peace talks were about the size and shape of the table around which the warring parties would gather. It was not a trivial consideration. It meant something.

Picture a rectangular table. There are places of honor (the "head of the table") and places of less honor. That is not true of a round table.

At a rectangular table, people square off opposite each other. Imagine a negotiation at a rectangular table. It is almost as if the table itself establishes the battle lines. That is not the case with a round table.

At a rectangular table, particularly a long one, you cannot see everyone else at the table, at least not fully—unless, of course, you are in the power seat at the head of the table. From that privileged perch, you can see everyone. At a round table, that privilege is afforded everyone. Every person can see every other person without obstruction.

Those are some of the reasons why a round table can be an instrument of reconciliation and an invitation to reconciliation as well.

I don't know the shape of the table around which Jesus would gather for meals with friends and strangers. If it were a rectangular table, we know he would refuse the place of honor. But I have a feeling he would have preferred a round table most of all.

Prayer

Welcome, Jesus, to the table. Make it a table of welcome and reconciliation. Amen.

Smells like Christ's Spirit

For we are the aroma of Christ to God among those who
are being saved and among those who are perishing.

—2 Corinthians 2:15

In scripture there are many descriptions of the kind of life we are called to live. One image the apostle Paul uses is that we are to be the "aroma of Christ."

It's a wonderful image. After all, the sense of smell has an immediacy to it beyond all the other senses. So when I smell a certain kind of wooden mustiness, it's not that I am reminded of the attic in the house in which I grew up, it is as if I am there. And I have to ask myself, "Why did I just think of that attic? Oh, yeah, it's that smell!" If I pass someone who is wearing the perfume my mother used to wear, I will turn around, half expecting to see my mother, even though she has been gone for a long time now.

To say that an aroma is a reminder or a stimulus for memory is to say too little. The aroma of something can transport you from the present moment and immediate surroundings to somewhere else entirely.

So Paul is saying, "You are to be like that. You are to be the aroma of Christ. By the way you infuse your daily encounters with love, by the way you forgive your enemies, by the way you care for the forgotten ones, you are to be that sweet aroma that seems to transport people into the very presence of Christ."

Is that a lot to expect? To be sure. But there is another way to put it: It is our high calling.

Prayer

Dear Jesus, infuse my life with your fragrance so that others might be ushered into your presence. Amen.

The Longing Heart

As a deer longs for flowing streams,
so my soul longs for you, O God.

—from Psalm 42

I am convinced that we all long for the presence of God with a deep, aching hunger, much as we hunger for food, but with this difference—we don't always know how to satisfy it. If we have a stomach hunger, we know that we need to eat some food. And, generally speaking, we have learned what constitutes nourishing food. We know, for instance, that if we are hungry, it will do us no good to fill our stomachs with cotton, or even cotton candy. We know that we need food—satisfying, nourishing food—in order to live.

But if we have a soul hunger, a spiritual yearning, we are not always sure how to fill it. And people will try almost anything to fill it, to take the ache away.

The philosopher Blaise Pascal once said that each one of us is born with an empty place in our hearts that is in the shape of God. This empty space is not a square hole, or anything as simple as that, but a complex, hungering, God-shaped space where only God fits, a space that only God can fill. We can try to fill that space with other things—human relationships, careers, or other earthly pursuits—but they will sooner or later leave us unsatisfied. After all, if that empty space implanted in our hearts is in the shape of God, then our attempts to fill it with anything else will leave empty corners that will continue to ache.

Before the fulfillment, there is the longing: "As a deer longs for flowing streams, so my soul longs for you, O God." Sometimes it is only after your hunger has been satisfied that you can see what you were hungry for all along.

Prayer

O God, my soul longs for you, even when I don't recognize that you are the object of my longing. Amen.

The Uses and Abuses of Anger

Be angry, but do not sin; do not let the
sun go down on your anger.
—from Ephesians 4:25–32

Of all the deadly sins, only anger is so precariously perched on the border of good and evil. We never speak of "righteous gluttony" or "just lust." But sometimes we speak of "righteous anger" or "just anger." Much of the great good in the world is achieved through anger.

Martin Luther extolled righteous anger as the engine that drove him on to some of his very best work. He wrote, "When I am angry I can write, pray, and preach well, for then my whole temperature is quickened, my understanding sharpened, and all mundane vexations and temptations depart."

But anger does not always enlarge our worldview and sharpen our insights. When anger takes over, our vision can become dangerously narrowed.

Anger can be the source of so much that is good and of so much that is evil. So how are we to make distinctions between the two?

Theologian Thomas Aquinas, writing in the fourteenth century, singled out three disordered expressions of anger:

First, when we get angry too easily.

Second, when we get more angry than we should. Some anger is simply disproportionate, out of scale with what prompts it.

Third, when we are angry for too long. We can hold onto our anger until it decays into a wretched mass of resentment and bitterness. The novelist Ann Lamott says that hanging onto resentments is like drinking rat poison and then waiting for the rat to die.

Paul's advice is even more succinct: "Do not let the sun go down on your anger."

Prayer

God, help me to make the tricky distinctions between righteous and self-righteous anger, between anger that serves and anger that is self-serving. Amen.

Enough Already

> Do not store up for yourselves treasures on
> earth, where moth and rust consume and
> where thieves break in and steal.
>
> —**Matthew 6:19**

When was it exactly that we began to need such big closets?

When my family lived in Phoenix, we had a comfortable home that was built in the early 1980s and, like most homes built in recent decades, it had very large closets—not large enough for Imelda Marcos's shoe collection, mind you, but plenty large enough for all the stuff we had.

When we moved to Massachusetts, we bought a house built in 1931. And, like most homes built in that era, it had small closets. This made unpacking a particular challenge. We simply did not have storage space for all our stuff.

How did we end up with all this stuff, anyway? And is that why so many houses are so large these days? After all, as the late comedian George Carlin put it, what is a house but a pile of all our stuff, with a cover on it? And we have a lot of stuff these days. So now the average American house is twice as big as it was fifty years ago, while in the same period family units became smaller.

How much stuff is enough? And how much space is enough to store it all?

For most of us, *enough* is defined as something more than what we have, a shifting standard that can be, and often is, adjusted upward.

I've never been to a dog track, but I'm pretty sure about one thing. I think I know the name of that wooden rabbit that keeps the panting pack running around the track. That rabbit's name is Enough. And whether it is a dog race or a rat race, no one ever seems to catch it.

Prayer

God, your creation is infused with your generosity. You take care of our every need. Quiet our hearts—and rebuke us—when we fear we do not have enough. Amen.

Titles Fancy and Plain

So which one is greater, the one who is seated
at the table or the one who serves at the table?
Isn't it the one who is seated at the table? But
I am among you as one who serves.

—Luke 22:27 CEB

Recently I have been thinking about titles and their significance.

For instance, the official title for the Queen of England is "Her Royal Highness, Elizabeth the Second, by the Grace of God, of Great Britain and Northern Ireland and of her other realms and territories Queen, Head of the Commonwealth, Defender of the Faith." Wow. Try fitting that title on a business card. Then again, if you are the Queen of England, you probably don't need a business card.

You don't have to be a monarch to get an exalted title. For example, fraternal organizations often use titles that are honorific. If you ascend the ranks of the Elks, eventually you can receive the title Exalted Ruler. Similarly, if you are a Shriner, you can become the Grand Potentate. Those are pretty fancy titles.

I once met General Wesley Clark, who had the title "NATO Supreme Allied Commander." That's quite a title. Later, I said to my family, "You know, I'd love to have a job where you get to have the word *Supreme* in your title."

I was only kidding, of course. I much prefer the titles given in church, which are considerably more modest. *Deacon* means servant. *Pastor* means shepherd. Both are modest roles associated with service and labor, and both are roles identified with Jesus. He was a servant and a shepherd.

And because Jesus was a servant, the highest honor is not to be given a medal or a gold watch. The highest honor is to be given a dish towel.

Prayer

Jesus, please show me how I am called to serve today, and then please glorify that service through your spirit. Amen.

The Psalmist Gets the Blues

My tears have been my food day and night.
—from Psalm 42

There are more prayers of lament in the Bible than there are prayers of praise. Fully one-third of the psalms are psalms of lament. Psalm 42 is one of them.

A biblical lament is an impassioned plea: "There is something wrong here. Things are not right. I must give voice to my complaint."

Lament is not whining. God does not like whiners. Whiners always find a way to whine, regardless of the circumstances, whereas lament is a legitimate response to hardship. The great Mahalia Jackson used to say, "Anybody singing the blues is in a deep pit, yelling for help." The same could be said of lament. The two have much in common.

I once asked a blues guitar player in my congregation to put this psalm to music. Sure enough, the words of the psalm and the agonized strains of the wailing guitar were a perfect match: "Tears have been my food, day and night."

Tears that are never shed do not go away. They become something else—bitterness, depression, hardness of heart, increased grief. We can offer lament in the confidence that God invites us to bring the fullness of our sorrow.

God receives our tears—the literal tears and the musical ones—as readily as God receives our songs of praise.

Prayer
Today I offer a prayer of thanksgiving that you invite our prayers of lament. Amen.

Whispered in Your Ear

And a voice from heaven said, "This is my Son,
the Beloved, with whom I am well pleased."
—from Matthew 3:13–17

According to a beautiful Muslim practice, as soon as a baby is born, the *adhan*—the call to prayer—is whispered into the baby's right ear. It begins, "*Allahu Akbar*"—which means, "Allah is great" or "God is great." So the word *God* is the first word a baby hears.

This is the same call to prayer that is issued five times a day. In Muslim areas, it echoes through the streets in a haunting chant. Wherever you are, whatever you are doing, the call to prayer finds you and, if you are Muslim, it is a reminder of what was first whispered in your ear when you were born. It strikes me as a powerful way of binding a child to God in the very first moments of life.

Jesus was an adult when he came to the waters of the Jordan to be baptized by John, but in Matthew's Gospel the story is told almost as if it were a second birth narrative. When Jesus emerged from the baptismal waters, dripping like an infant fresh from the womb, the Spirit of God descended upon him and a voice from heaven said, "You are my Son, the Beloved; my favor rests on you."

That, in essence, is what we whisper in the ear of anyone who comes to be baptized: "You are God's beloved." Those are the first words we hear. That is who we are. It is good to be reminded of that. At least five times a day.

Prayer

Holy Spirit, help me to look past the many voices that seek to tell me who I am and what I am worth, so that I might hear again what was whispered in my ear at baptism: "You are my beloved." Amen.

Cake or Death?

> I call heaven and earth to witness against you today that
> I have set before you life and death, blessings and curses.
> Choose life so that you and your descendants may live.
>
> **—Deuteronomy 30:19**

The comedian Eddie Izzard has a classic routine in which he imagines how the Inquisition would have been conducted if the Church of England had been in charge. He imagines the Anglican priests being far too genteel to torture their victims. They are too fond of tea and cakes for anything as gruesome as that. So, instead, they offer prisoners a choice: "Cake or death?" It all seems to go swimmingly until every single person being interrogated chooses the cake. "Well, we've run out of cake," says the exasperated priest. The prisoner responds, "So what is my choice? Or death?"

When we read this passage from Deuteronomy in a superficial way, it can sound a lot like that routine. Given the choice between life and death, wouldn't we always choose life? After all, with life comes cake, as well as many other delights.

But sometimes the choice is not nearly as clear. For instance, when I was a young boy, our neighbors dug a hole in their backyard for a swimming pool. The whole neighborhood was crackling with anticipation.

Then came the Cuban missile crisis. The neighbors began to rethink their plans. Should they build a bomb shelter instead of a swimming pool? Should they trade in their dream of frolicking in the sun for the assurance of safety underground? And which decision would be choosing life?

Eventually, they decided to use the hole in their backyard to build a bomb shelter. They thought that, in making this decision, they were choosing life. In retrospect, it seems clear that they gave death the upper hand. Fear can do that.

Prayer

God, guide me in my decisions today that I might rightly discern which is the path to life. Amen.

I Don't Envy You

You shall not covet your neighbor's house;
you shall not covet your neighbor's wife, or
male or female slave, or ox, or donkey, or
anything that belongs to your neighbor.
—**Exodus 20:17**

A new term has come into common parlance these days: *Facebook envy*. Researchers have found, and many people have experienced, that spending time on Facebook can make people more envious. Viewing all your friends' fabulous vacations, lovely children, and great social lives can leave you feeling lonely, frustrated, and angry. It is a manifestation of the tendency we have of comparing our inner realities with other people's outer appearances.

We are keenly aware of what is really going on in our lives and it cannot measure up to what we see on the surface of others' lives. Such asymmetrical comparisons can easily stir envy.

Facebook seems to promise intimacy, or at least close proximity to others—but that is part of the problem. Envy tends to do its work most easily, most destructively, at close range. The philosopher Søren Kierkegaard called envy a small-town sin because it is a by-product of living in such close proximity that we are constantly tempted to make invidious comparisons. So most of us don't spend much time envying the super rich. Instead, as H. L. Mencken once put it, in America, happiness is making ten dollars more a month than your brother-in-law.

The opposite of envy is gratitude—gratitude for the gifts you have been given. Among these are the gift of life and the particular life that is yours to live, and the unique talents you have been blessed with. Envy cannot grow in a thankful heart. Envy and gratitude are always competing for our souls.

Prayer

God, as much as possible, root out envy from my heart and replace it with gratitude. Amen.

Secret Giving

When you give to the poor, do not let your left
hand know what your right hand is doing,
so that your giving may be in secret.

—Matthew 6:3–4 NASB

While a friend and I were waiting at the counter for our coffee, he asked, "Do you wait to put something in the tip jar until the barista can see you doing it?"

My friend went on to explain that he always makes sure that the person serving him sees that he is leaving a tip. But he questions his own motives. "On the one hand, it could be that I am just trying to get credit for leaving a tip (and I usually do get a nice 'thank you' in return). But on the other hand, the tip is also a way of expressing appreciation—and that is an interaction between two individuals. How can that interaction take place if she doesn't see me put my tip in the tip jar?"

To be sure, this is not one of the most pressing ethical issues of our time, but it is another example of our ambivalence about giving and secrecy. In church I have heard (and have probably said myself on occasion), "Your giving is only between you and your God." Really? Is giving an entirely private matter? What is the role of community and covenant?

Most of us are quite good at justifying our approach to money. So if you are inclined to seek privacy in giving, consider that you may be trying to avoid accountability. And if you are public in giving, consider that you may be looking for praise. Hard to get it right? Of course. We are talking about money here.

Prayer

God, help me to think clearly about money—clearly enough to know that it is most appropriate to begin with confession. Amen.

Playing Old Tapes

> All who heard [Paul] were amazed and said, "Is
> not this the man who made havoc in Jerusalem
> among those who invoked this name?"
>
> **—from Acts 9:19–22**

Before our two children were both married, my wife and I suggested we take a trip together as a family. This was a special treat because opportunities for the four of us to travel together were becoming increasingly rare. In the harried swirl of last-minute activity that always seems to precede a trip, I chased our daughter, Alanna, with these words as she ran up the stairs: "Please finish packing so that we can leave on time, okay?"

In response, Alanna walked down a few stairs and, with a steady gaze from her perch there, said in a deliberate manner, "Dad, when was the last time I was late in getting ready for a trip? I haven't done that in years. You're playing old tapes. Besides, I've finished packing. And I'm the only one."

Immediately I knew that she was right. She had changed, but I had not changed my perception. I apologized and finished my own packing, duly chastened.

The apostle Paul started out as a persecutor of Christians, but then, after an encounter with the risen Christ, he became a Christian himself. He was a changed person. But the people around him were skeptical. They couldn't believe that he had actually changed, and they had difficulty letting him be that changed person.

It can seem as if people never really change, at least not in any fundamental way. But sometimes it just seems that way because, in our perceptions, we have not allowed them to change. Do you have some "old tapes" that you need to discard today?

Prayer

God, I find it difficult to change. And sometimes I find it difficult to recognize the change that has taken place in my life or the lives of those around me. Please enlighten the eyes of my heart so that I might recognize your transformative grace in and around me. Amen.

The Surprising Samaritan

Which of these three, do you think, proved to be a
neighbor to the man who fell among the robbers?
—from Luke 10:25–37 CEB

One summer when I was a youth minister for a small church
in rural Connecticut, one of my responsibilities was to work
with the children and youth while their parents were in worship.

One week we gave the parable of the Good Samaritan a
decidedly modern twist. I parked my car on the shoulder of the
road to give the impression that it was disabled.

Most of the young people hid behind bushes in a nearby
field, clutching flowers and cards that said, "Thank you; you
are a Good Samaritan," waiting to shower these gifts upon the
good souls who stopped to help me.

I kept two children with me by the car. I chose these two
because, although most children are accomplished at turning
on a pathetic look at a moment's notice, these two clearly were
masters of the art.

Car after car passed without stopping. Everyone was getting
restless. I began to wonder how I could salvage some lesson in
this unexpected turn of events.

Finally, when worship was almost over, a station wagon
pulled over. A woman I did not recognize got out of the car and
exclaimed, "Tim! What's going on?" One of the young people
beside me replied, "Mom!" It seems she had just finished her
shopping and was heading back to the church to pick up her son.

Tim hugged his mother. Multitudes appeared from the
bushes with exultant cheers and gave her every bouquet and a
stack of cards.

I did not have the heart to tell them that what happened that
morning was precisely *not* what the parable of the Good Samaritan is about. It is not about coming to the aid of those we know.

In Jesus's day, Samaritans and Jews did not have any dealings with one another. Among all those who saw the injured Jew, the Samaritan had the best reason of all to say, "What has that to do with me?" But this Samaritan did not see a stranger or an enemy. This Samaritan saw another child of God, a neighbor. That is what makes the Samaritan's charity so remarkable.

Prayer

God, give me a generosity of heart that does not ask, "What has that to do with me?" Amen.

Christmas Is a Surprise Party

About that day or hour no one knows. . . . Beware, keep
alert; for you do not know when the time will come.

—from Mark 13:24–37

In a way it is unfortunate that we always celebrate Christmas
on the same day of the year, because that makes the coming of
Christ seem almost predictable. But Christmas is more like a
surprise party.

For centuries God's people awaited the coming of the
Promised One. Then, when it happened, most people missed
it. They were watching the ceremonial gates, and he snuck in
the servants' entrance.

God is always slipping into town when we least expect it,
and where we least expect it as well, even in the darkest time of
year, in a forgotten corner, as a baby with milk on its breath.

Although December 25 is fixed on the calendar, we never
know when the Spirit of Christ will be born in our midst. Our
task is to live with an air of expectation, because it could be any
time, even today, and anywhere, even here.

A friend tells about asking a group what keeps them coming
to church. Someone responded, "It's strange, I know, but I get the
feeling here, like nowhere else, that something is about to happen."

What a great description! In the church, we gather around
the expectation that something is about to happen. And we may
even be able to affirm that it's Jesus, the Spirit of Christ, that
is about to happen. But we don't know when. We don't know
where. We don't know how. So we wait with bated breath, and
our souls atingle, for the surprise party to begin.

Prayer
God, keep me awake, by whatever means necessary, so I won't
miss your surprise party when it begins. Amen.

Remember Your Baptism

After this Jesus and his disciples went into
the Judean countryside, and he spent some
time there with them and baptized.

—from John 3:22–36

Martin Luther, the great reformer, was clearly a genius and a person of great faith, but he was also something of a tormented soul. Among other maladies, he suffered from what would be called clinical depression today. Out of those depths, he affirmed that there is no greater comfort than baptism. In dark times, he would remind himself: "I am baptized. And through my baptism the God who cannot lie has bound himself to me." Particularly when he did not feel worthy of another person's love, he clung to the tangible expression of God's love in baptism.

Someone confided about the experience of growing up as a teenager with a terrible case of acne. When she looked into the mirror each morning, she would recoil from what she saw. But then she would splash water on her face and, in the words spoken at Jesus's baptism and echoed in her own baptism, she would say, "I am beloved." In the soapy water of her sink she was able to seek comfort and strength in the recollection of the promise of her baptism.

What do you see when you look in the mirror? Do you see lines of anxiety or anger or blemishes of some kind? Do you like what you see? If you are not entirely pleased with the one who looks back at you in the mirror, remember your baptism. In that act, the God who cannot lie has called you beloved.

Prayer
Ever-loving, never-lying God, thank you for the promise of my baptism and for calling me beloved, even when I feel unlovable. Amen.

A Silly Question?

Jesus stood still and ordered the [blind] man to be brought to him; and when he came near, he asked him, "What do you want me to do for you?"

—from Luke 18:35–43

When a blind man cries out to Jesus as he passes by on the road to Jericho, Jesus responds by asking him, "What do you want me to do for you?"

Is that a silly question? I mean, if you are blind, of course what you want most of all is to have your sight restored. Does Jesus have to ask?

But we have to be careful here. Most of us have a tendency to assume that we know what another person needs or wants, particularly if that person is dealing with some kind of challenge or disability.

Perhaps what the blind man wants, more than anything else in the world, is something other than the restoration of his sight. He might respond to Jesus's question by saying, "What I most want is to be reconciled with my father" or "I want to share my life with someone." One of those, or something else entirely, might be his deepest yearning. You will only know if you ask.

So when Jesus asks, "What do you want me to do for you?" he is showing respect for the man. He is not presuming to know what he wants. He is asking. And he is listening.

Prayer

O God, help me to respond to the needs of people without presuming to know what those needs are. Give me the wisdom to ask and to listen. Amen.

Welcome Home

My refuge and my fortress;
my God, in whom I trust.
—from Psalm 91

*H*ome. It is hard to think of another word with as many deep resonances. Whether we are responding to the presence or the absence of something called home, the word itself seems to echo in the deeper recesses of our hearts.

A home is so much more than a house. A home is a place, or a dream of a place, where you feel uniquely *at home*, which is to say a place where you feel that you belong.

Some of us have an actual place like that, a place that comforts and enfolds, a place where we can seek refuge from the world and are refreshed to face the world again. Whether you live alone or with others, it is a place where you don't have to explain everything. It is a place where you can be yourself, for better or worse, and usually it is both. And, in the home of our dreams, at least, it is a place where you feel accepted, loved even. There are not many places like that in the world, and we all need such a place.

The authors of scripture talk about God in some of the same ways, as a shelter and a comfort, as the one who accepts us just as we are, who enfolds us with care and equips us to serve. Perhaps that is why scripture speaks of God as a home. "God is my refuge and my fortress," writes the psalmist, using the words that would later inspire Martin Luther's famous hymn "A Mighty Fortress." Elsewhere we read, "Lord, you have been our dwelling place in all generations." Imagine: God is our home.

Whether the home in which you live is a sanctuary or roiled with conflict, grand or plain, a real place or merely the stuff of dreams, we all have the same gracious home in God. So welcome home.

Prayer

O God, thank you that you have been our refuge, our dwelling place, throughout all generations and are so even now and even for me. Amen.

He Had a Name

There was a rich man who was dressed in purple and
fine linen and who feasted sumptuously every day.
And at his gate lay a poor man named Lazarus.

—from Luke 16:19–31

Jesus begins this parable, "There was a rich man . . ." The rich man's name is not given, which should tip us off from the beginning that something unusual is going on here, because rich people's names generally are known and known quite well. If you are rich, it seems that everyone knows your name. The names of rich people are spoken like magic words. Those names have the power to open closed doors. And yet Jesus gives no name to the rich man in the parable.

It is safe to assume that the rich man of the parable does not know the name of the beggar who sits at the gate of his house. But in the parable the beggar has a name—Lazarus, a name that means "God helps." It is a rather poignant name, for clearly no one but God made an effort to help him. It is the only time Jesus ever uses a name in a parable. To the rich man, the beggar is nameless, just a person to be ignored, invisible. But to God, he has a name. He is not known as "a beggar." He is Lazarus.

Like so many of Jesus's teachings, this parable upends the usual order of things. In the world, rich men's names are known and beggars are often treated as nameless. In the parable, as in God's realm, it is the beggar, of all people, who is addressed by name.

Prayer
I am not very good with names, God. But you are. Thank you for knowing me—and each person—by name. Amen.

God Knows Already. So Why Pray?

Your Father knows what you need before you ask him.
—from Matthew 6:5–15

Jesus said that God knows our prayers even before we utter them. That affirmation leads to an obvious question: If God knows all of that already, what is the point of prayer?

Well, imagine a couple who have been married for many years. In spite of all they have been through together—or is it *because* of all they have been through together?—they love each other still. But one night, over coffee and dessert, the husband is obviously disturbed about something. The wife knows to wait. It will come out eventually. And, sure enough, he starts out, "You know, it occurred to me today that you never tell me that you love me anymore."

The wife responds, "Oh, you know I love you. Very much."

"Yes."

"Then why do I have to say it?"

"Because it makes a difference. I need to hear it even when I know what you are going to say before you say it."

So, yes, God knows our prayers even before we utter them, but we need to offer them anyway. It makes a difference. Saying the words themselves creates tender ties. Words of love are never unnecessary, never redundant, and neither are words of prayer. A silent understanding cannot replace a loving exchange of words, even familiar words, or words that are known before they are spoken.

Prayer

God, I invite you to take a tour of my heart and mind, to see all that resides there—my half-formed thoughts, my yearnings, my confessions. And give me the words to speak. Give me the words. Amen.

Being Available 24/6

And if the peoples of the land bring in merchandise
or any grain on the sabbath day to sell, we will not
buy it from them on the sabbath or on a holy day.

—**Nehemiah 10:31**

When I was a student in divinity school, one Saturday my best friend and I drove to Manhattan to buy an engagement ring. (He had gotten engaged the year before, so clearly he was an expert in this area.) I had grown up outside of New York, so I was familiar with the famous Diamond District—47th Street, between Fifth and Sixth Avenues. On an average day, $400 million of jewelry is sold on that one city block. It has something of the feel of an exotic and teeming bazaar, with people loudly bustling from store to store. Some are dressed in ties and suits, while many others wear the long black frocks of Hasidic Jews and different styles of black hats, each style characteristic of a different Hasidic group. In the entire city, perhaps only the floor of the New York Stock Exchange has more of a sense of concentrated commercial energy.

When we turned the corner onto 47th Street, I immediately knew something was wrong. There was no bustle of activity. No loud clamoring of commerce. No lights in the stores.

The reason, of course, was that it was Saturday, the Jewish Sabbath. There would be no working, no buying, no selling—at least, not on that block, not on that day. These people of faith will make themselves available 24/6 but not 24/7, because the seventh day is hallowed as the Sabbath.

I said to my friend, "Don't they want my money?" And he replied, "I'm sure they do. But they want to be good Jews even more."

I think of the opening lines of the famous William Wordsworth poem:

The world is too much with us; late and soon,
Getting and spending, we lay waste our powers.

In keeping the Sabbath, we are free for a time from those things that "lay waste our powers."

Prayer

God, even if my work is not yet done, let me rest as if the work is done. Amen.

The Ever-Present God

Even though I walk through the darkest
valley, I fear no evil; for you are with me; your
rod and your staff—they comfort me.

—Psalm 23:4

Psalm 23 contains the first verses of scripture many of us commit to memory. In a way it is odd that we would teach this psalm to children, because it speaks of realities that most children have yet to confront fully—"the darkest valley," evil, and enemies. So when we teach children this psalm, we are giving them a gift that may take them a lifetime to appreciate fully. Memorize this, we say, bury it deep in your consciousness, and mark well where you left it, because someday you will need it. Sooner or later, you will need it urgently.

I once heard about a species of bird that migrates over huge expanses of water carrying a twig in its beak, so that when the storms come it can float on the water, kept from drowning by the twig. And so this psalm has been for many people when the storms come, as they inevitably do on our long journeys.

The words of this psalm also are the last words many people hear. I have recited them at countless bedsides, including times when a person who had seemingly lost all consciousness moved her lips to silently form the familiar words and taste them one more time.

It is fitting that these words accompany us from the beginning of our lives until the end, because the words themselves speak of God's everlasting presence with us. The everlasting psalm is an audible reminder of the ever-present God.

Prayer
God, I praise you as you accompany me throughout my days
and even as I walk through the darkest valley. Amen.

Jesus Goes to Hell

My God, my God, why have you forsaken me?
—Psalm 22:1

To be sure, I have never experienced the kind of suffering Jesus endured on the cross, but you do not have to experience pain on that scale to ask God, as Jesus did, "Why have you forsaken me?" Life being what it is, at one time or another, in one form or another, everyone has occasion to ask that question. What Jesus's question says to me is that even my feelings of being abandoned by God are not foreign to God.

The Apostle's Creed contains this affirmation about Jesus: "Jesus Christ was crucified, dead and buried. He descended to hell." The last part of that statement always used to trouble me, until one day someone told me that, for her, it is the most treasured part of the creed. When I asked why, she answered, "Because hell is where I spend much of my life." Hell—a sense of being forsaken, the absence of God, a place of despair. We have been there. And Jesus has been there. And having been there, Jesus transformed it.

One who would rescue those trapped in a mine shaft sometimes must enter into the danger and darkness of that place himself. How else can those who are trapped be saved, if the one who knows the way out is not willing to come to them?

I am grateful that Jesus is willing to enter our darkness so that he might usher us into the light. So even this word of despair from the cross ends up being good news indeed.

Prayer

Holy One, thank you for your willingness to share in human defeat, so that we might, in turn, share in your victory. Amen.

God Has Many Names

How often have I desired to gather your children
together as a hen gathers her brood under her wings.
—from Luke 13:31–35

What's your favorite name for God? There are so many choices. The Bible contains dozens of names for God.

Some names remind us that God is powerful and mysterious: I Am, Alpha and Omega, Sun of Righteousness, Bright Morning Star, Ancient of Days, Holy One.

Other names seem to bring God to our side in an intimate way: *Abba* (which means "Papa" or "Daddy"), Comforter, Counselor, Love. During Advent, we particularly call upon God in Christ with the name Emmanuel, which means "God with us."

Many of the names for God in the Bible are masculine, but others, like the name in our reading today (Brooding Hen) are feminine, and still others are gender neutral.

Why do we have so many names for God? Quite simply, each name says something about God, but not all that can be said. No one name is sufficient. So we draw on a rich treasure trove of many names. As one beautiful hymn charges us, "Bring many names, beautiful and good."

So what is your favorite name for God? May I suggest that you use that name now to call upon God in prayer.

Prayer

I know you by many names, but the name that seems to draw me closest to you is _____. Thank you for giving me a name with which to address you, because that means that you long to be in relationship with me. Amen.

Rewriting Your Obituary

You fool! This very night your life is
being demanded of you.
—from Luke 12:13–21

During much of his life, Alfred Nobel, the Swedish scientist and inventor, was best known for the invention of dynamite. In 1888, Alfred's brother Ludwig died while visiting France, and one French newspaper mistakenly reported that it was Alfred Nobel, and not his brother, who had died. They ran an obituary for Alfred Nobel under the headline, "The Merchant of Death Is Dead." The first line of his obituary was this: "Dr. Alfred Nobel, who became rich by finding ways to kill more people faster than ever before, died yesterday."

So Alfred Nobel had the unique opportunity to read his own obituary. And he was horrified that his life could be summarized in such a way, that devising an explosive as destructive as dynamite was the sum of his life, that this, of all things, was what he would be remembered for.

That incident left a lasting impression on Nobel. He became determined to leave a better legacy. So seven years after his obituary appeared in that French newspaper, Nobel signed papers that stipulated that the bulk of his estate would be used to establish the Nobel Prizes, including, of course, the Nobel Peace Prize. In a sense, he had a chance to rewrite his obituary, and he took full advantage of the opportunity.

But, come to think of it, we are all writing our own obituaries by the way we live our lives, aren't we? Our obituaries are being written every day.

Prayer
Craft in me, O God, a life worth living, one day at a time, one act at a time. Amen.

Don't Try This at Home

Praise the Lord! I will give thanks to the
Lord with my whole heart, in the company
of the upright, in the congregation.

—Psalm 111:1

Marjorie Scoboria, one of the beloved saints of the last congregation I served, died just short of her 104th birthday. The Sunday before her death, she was in her usual spot in the congregation: the fourteenth row on the left. (Did you think preachers don't notice that sort of thing?) She was offering her witty little quips to those around her and standing for the hymns.

In other ways, however, she was limited in how she could participate. In recent years, her eyesight and her hearing were almost completely gone, but she continued to come to worship every Sunday. When I asked Marjorie about that (after all, if I were over a hundred years old, I think I would stay in bed every once in a while on a Sunday), she looked surprised by the question and replied, "Because I need to be in the congregation with the people."

It is almost proverbial that "ninety percent of life is just showing up." But that's wrong. Ninety percent of life is showing up over and over again.

People sometimes speak of "going to church" on Sunday morning as if the church had some kind of existence without the people, or as if it were merely a building.

We all know the children's game that says, "Here is the church, here is the steeple, open the doors and see all the people." That may be a good game, but it is bad theology. As Marjorie knew so well, the church *is* the people. So you have to show up. It's not church until you get there.

Prayer

God, thank you for the saints in our congregation—the ones who show us how it is done. Amen.

God's Holy Fools

Do you have eyes, and fail to see?
Do you have ears, and fail to hear?
—from Mark 8:14–21

I have always identified with the disciples as they are depicted in Mark's Gospel. Far from holy and wholly together, they are the original gang that couldn't shoot straight, fumbling and fickle, often missing the point. In fact, the first sermon I preached after I was ordained was on this passage, and I picked up on these themes. My sermon was titled "God's Holy Fool," which was my description of the original disciples. Unfortunately, I didn't think about how that title would look on the board outside the church:

GOD'S HOLY FOOL
MARTIN B. COPENHAVER PREACHING

In this passage, Jesus is speaking to his disciples after the multiplication of loaves and fishes. They were present when the crowds were fed. They had picked up the baskets of scraps that were left over after all the people had their fill. But when Jesus asks them to recall what happened, they simply report the facts: five loaves for five thousand people and twelve baskets of scraps. Jesus had given them a stunning glimpse of God's power and all they could see or remember was a hillside picnic.

I wouldn't be so dim-witted. *I* wouldn't miss a miracle like that. But then I remember that the word *miracle* literally means "sign that points to God." So, yes, I am still one of God's holy fools, because I am quite sure that I miss miracles—signs that point to God—every day.

Prayer
Jesus, thank you that you love me and claim me as your own, even when I am being a dim-witted fool. Amen.

The Stuff of God

> Then he said, "I will do this: I will pull down
> my barns and build larger ones, and there I
> will store all my grain and my goods."
>
> —from Luke 12:13–21

Not long ago, my wife and I moved from a ten-room house, with an attic and a basement as bulging as chipmunk cheeks, to a four-room apartment. Neck-deep in the detritus of our lives, of course we concluded that we had too much. How did I end up with two drawers and two large bins of T-shirts? Did we really need a food processor, a mini–food processor, and two blenders (including one that doesn't work, for . . . what? spare parts?). At least we didn't get a storage unit, like the farmer in Jesus's parable, who wanted to store all his crops.

No wonder there are best-selling books on how to declutter and television shows about helping hoarders. We are drowning in stuff. But, as George Carlin put it, "Do you notice how everyone else's stuff is junk, but your junk is *stuff*?"

Some stuff is not exactly stuff, but something more. For instance, the Best Chicken Feeder Award, given to our son at his preschool, which was a working farm. How could we possibly get rid of that? Or how about the ceramic figurine of a cardinal? I would never pick it out at a store or choose to make room for it except that my mother, who is now long gone, loved birds—and this figurine—beyond reason. Or the two RSV Bibles, identical in every way, except one was given to me in third grade and the other after we moved across the country to another church in fourth grade? I do not want to dispense with either one.

As Christians, people of the Incarnation, we affirm in various ways that God resides in stuff—in all stuff in some way, in some stuff in particular. I don't need to be reminded of that—I experience it as we declutter.

Prayer

In confronting my stuff, help me be open to a surprise encounter with you. Amen.

Baptizing Newborns of Any Age

On hearing this, they were baptized
in the name of the Lord Jesus.
—from Acts 19:1–7

In my denomination, we do not have a normative age for baptism. So I have baptized infants who are just weeks old, and I once baptized a man who was eighty-seven. Somehow the waters of baptism make newborns out of us all.

One of the things I love about baptizing infants, however, is that it is clear that this is a sacrament of grace. A baby cannot earn baptism or in any way deserve it.

Before an adult is baptized, he is asked to affirm faith in the God we know in Jesus Christ. That can mistakenly lead us to believe that we have to do something first before God can act in the sacrament.

In baptizing infants, we recognize that baptism is not about anything we do. Before an infant can affirm any faith in God, God binds God's own self to her. Nothing she has done prepared her to receive that gift; nothing she has failed to do prevents her from receiving it.

Some people approach worship as the place where God adds to their to-do lists. We come distracted by our own to-do list, and God adds "Seek justice" or "Pray more" or "Serve a meal at the homeless shelter."

But worship is not primarily about what we are supposed to do. It is primarily about what God has already done. When baptismal waters trickle off the nose of an infant and we declare that in that act she is bound to God, we understand that we are not the primary actors in this drama. Our to-do lists are not the central focus. Instead, we see that we were on God's to-do list all along.

Prayer

God, give me words of praise for all you have done, because you acted even before I had a chance to do anything, anything at all. Amen.

Strong at the Broken Places

Whenever I am weak, then I am strong.
—2 Corinthians 12:10

Ernest Hemingway sounds very much like the apostle Paul when he writes in *A Farewell to Arms*, "The world breaks every one and afterward many are strong at the broken places."

As Christians, however, we understand our brokenness and become strong in a particular way. Paul affirms that, for the Christian, all of life is a reenactment of the death and resurrection of Jesus. His story is not just one we can hear; it is also a story in which we are invited to share.

The world may break everyone, but that is not the last word. The Christian does not hold that things always turn out for the best, for they seldom do. Rather, we affirm that, through it all, God loves us, upholds us, receives us.

That is because our God is the kind of God who insists on having the last word. To be sure, the second to last word, which may be very powerful, can be given to something else—suffering, despair, hopelessness, evil, death itself. But our God insists on having the very last word, and that is always a helpful word, a healing word, a word of peace, of hopefulness, and of life.

That is what it means to participate in the death and resurrection of Jesus. It is about God taking the raw stuff of defeat and forging an ultimate victory. It is about becoming strong at the broken places.

Prayer
God, thank you for the promise that my life is so bound to Jesus's life that, even when I am broken, I can become strong at the broken places. Amen.

Don't Judge

Therefore you have no excuse, whoever you
are, when you judge others; for in passing
judgment on another you condemn yourself.

—from Romans 2:1–11

Throughout scripture God is described as both a God of judgment and a God of love. They are both defining characteristics of God.

It is important to note, however, that at every turn we are invited to reflect God's love in our relationships with one another and at no point are we asked to take on God's role of judge. In fact, we are warned against it. We must love as God loves. But we must not judge. That role is for God alone. That is because we are imperfect beings. All of us love imperfectly, but wonderful things can still be done through imperfect love. By contrast, imperfect judgment is dangerous. It can lead to ruptured relationships, prejudice, even violence.

That is why judgments we are forced to make—such as when someone is on trial for a crime—are to be made with modesty and humility. All human judgments are provisional, waiting upon the perfect judgment that is God's alone. Human frailty does not allow for more.

So love extravagantly today, in the name of the God of love. But, as far as you are able, hold back on your judgments and leave that role to God.

Prayer

God, you know I am tempted to judge others. I assume I can see others clearly. Give me humility to hold back my judgment. Amen.

Life or Death? You Choose

See, I have set before you today life and
prosperity, death and adversity.
—**Deuteronomy 30:15**

People of faith and faith communities can play a crucial role in addressing the environmental crisis. That does not mean we will, however.

There is a story about a Zen master who is known for his wisdom, for always having the right answer to difficult questions. Then comes a day when one of his prideful disciples decides to challenge the master. He holds a small bird in his closed hand and asks, "Master, is the bird alive or dead?"

The question is intended to be a trap. If the master says that the bird is alive, the disciple can merely crush it in his hand, place the bird at the feet of the master, and say, "No, you are wrong. The bird is dead." And if the master says, "The bird is dead," the disciple can then prove the master wrong by opening his hand and letting the bird fly away. The master pauses; he repeats the question: "Is the bird alive or dead?" And then he adds: "It is as you will."

It seems to me that also is the appropriate answer, and perhaps the only answer, to the question "Is our earthly home as we know it on its way to extinction or to new life?"

"It is as you will," says our Master.

Prayer

Creator God, show us ways—real and concrete ways—we can choose the way of life rather than death, both for ourselves and for your creation. Amen.

Come On In, the Water's Fine

Finally, he took me to the inside
court of the Temple of God.
—**Ezekiel 8:16 MSG**

Have you noticed that most people, when they come to worship, don't sit up front? The back of the church tends to fill up first, almost as predictably as the bottom of a glass will be the first to be filled with water. Why is that? If we were attending a concert or a lecture, we would charge down front where the "good seats" are. But why not when we come to worship?

I have heard a number of theories for this phenomenon. People want to be able to see who else is there, which is easier to do from the back. And it is easier to slip out quickly after worship if you sit in the back.

Those explanations may be part of the story, but I have another theory. I think we don't immediately go to the front because that would feel like a definitive declaration of faith. Sitting in the back, you can still feel as if you have one foot in and one foot out. To stride down the aisle and sit in the front feels like skipping right to the "your whole self in" part of the hokey pokey, and we may not be ready for that. Our own experience of faith often is more qualified, more tentative than that.

If doubt or uncertainty disqualifies us from worship, we will have many empty churches. Some of us live lives of doubt, diversified by faith. Others of us live a life of faith, diversified by doubt. And in the church there is room for us all. Even at the front.

In the Temple in Jerusalem, there was an inner court, reserved for the righteous, and an outer court for everyone else. I am grateful that, in the congregations of which I have been a part, it is all an inner court and all are invited there—no matter who you are.

Prayer

Thank you, God, that your invitation to me is not based on my righteousness, but instead flows from your graciousness. Amen.

Reading a Love Letter

> Now there was an Ethiopian eunuch, a court official
> of the Candace, queen of the Ethiopians, in charge
> of her entire treasury. He had come to Jerusalem
> to worship and was returning home; seated in his
> chariot, he was reading the prophet Isaiah.
>
> **—from Acts 8:26–40**

You have to really want to read something to read it in a moving chariot. After all, roads were rough in those days and shock absorbers had not yet been invented. But here is this Ethiopian eunuch returning home from a pilgrimage to Jerusalem, reading from the prophet Isaiah while riding in his chariot. Why was he so engrossed?

Well, the passage he was reading declares God's special love for those who are mistreated and ostracized. This comes as very good news to the eunuch, because he knows something about those conditions. As a eunuch, he was not even allowed inside the Temple, because he was considered unclean. He had been the perpetual outsider, but now he is reading about how God holds him and others who are rejected particularly close.

In his classic *How to Read a Book*, the philosopher Mortimer Adler wrote this:

> There is only one situation I can think of in which men and women make an effort to read better than they usually do. When they are in love and reading a love letter, they read for all they are worth. They read every word three ways; they read between the lines and in the margins. They may even take the punctuation into account. Then, if never before or after, they read.

That is why the eunuch is so engrossed in what he is reading. It is as if he is reading a love letter addressed to him and to all

191

who have known rejection. No wonder he is reading for all he is worth.

Prayer

God, next time I read the Bible, inspire me to read for all I am worth, as if reading a love letter, because . . . well, that's what it is. Amen.

Searchlights and Penlights

The discerning person looks to wisdom, but the
eyes of the fool to the ends of the earth.
—**Proverbs 17:24**

Sister Helen Prejean, the Roman Catholic nun who wrote the
book *Dead Man Walking*, said in a lecture, "I'm always asking
God for a searchlight. But, instead, God gives me a penlight."

I nodded my head because that has been my experience as
well. I am always looking for the searchlight that lets me see
every turn in the road and how the journey ends, even before
I start. You see, I am a planner by nature. I'm the guy who
carries around a multiyear calendar that includes events or com-
mitments three years from now. I want to see as far ahead as I
possibly can. So, in one way or another, I am always asking for
a searchlight.

Instead, most of the time, God gives me something more
like a penlight, which offers just enough illumination to see
where I can plant my foot next—but no more. Walking by
penlight forces a person to be patient with the unknown and to
exercise a bit of trust. And that can be challenging.

Even when I was young, I wanted the searchlight and had
to learn how to walk by penlight. When I, or another member of my family of origin, was consumed with a decision and
uncertain as to how to proceed, my mother would say, "When
the time comes, it will be clear." When I was young, I resisted
her counsel. I had difficulty with the "when the time comes"
part and, to be honest, I still do. How about now? What's wrong
with now?

Now that I am older, however, when I am impatient with
the slow unfolding of events, I can still hear my mother's voice
say, "When the time comes, it will be clear." And, over time,
I've learned that she was right.

Prayer

God, if I can't have the searchlight, show me how to walk by penlight. Amen.

The Sacred Blur Brought into Focus

For the cloud of the Lord was on the tabernacle
by day, and fire was in the cloud by night.
—from Exodus 40:34–38

In this passage, the presence of God is described as a cloud. That image reminds me of a parishioner's description of his concept of God as "a sacred blur."

When we recognize God in Jesus, however, that sacred blur is brought into stark, startling focus. We see what God is like and how we are to live in response to God's claim on our lives.

Some Christian traditions, including my own, often seem to speak more easily of God than of Jesus. Perhaps this stems from the difficulty we have in believing all that is claimed about Jesus. But I think the opposite often is the case. Our uneasiness with Jesus may not derive from our doubt that God was in Jesus in a unique way. Rather, our uneasiness may flow from our suspicion that it may be true after all. If it is true, then we must confront God and confront ourselves more fully, and who feels entirely prepared for that?

It can be easier, and perhaps less demanding, to think of God as something blurrier, like a cloud. When God has a human face, and lives the kind of life we do, we are given the opportunity—and the challenge—to see what a life claimed by God actually looks like.

Prayer

Sweet and precious Lord, may we see in you both something of God and something of ourselves, so that your life might shape our own. Amen.

The Miracle of Multiplication

And all ate and were filled; and they took up twelve
baskets full of broken pieces and of the fish. Those
who had eaten the loaves numbered five thousand.

—from Mark 6:30–44

According to one interpretation of the multiplication of the loaves and fishes, the people who gathered to be with Jesus brought their own food with them but, out of self-concern and the fear that they did not have enough, they hid it from others. They kept it their pockets. Then, according to this interpretation, when they saw Jesus offer them whatever meager scraps of food he had, the people were moved to a more generous impulse, reached into their pockets, and shared whatever they had brought. And in so doing they found it was enough. It was more than enough.

I am not drawn to this interpretation, because we live in a scientific age that is skeptical of anything supernatural. If God wanted to multiply loaves and fishes—or even make those fish waltz in three-quarter time, for that matter—God could do that.

But is it any less a miracle if this interpretation is true? Given the way that self-concern and fear grip the human heart, is it any less a sign of God's presence if, for once, we escape their hold on us?

And if that is the real miracle, it is not just a miracle we see Jesus perform; it is a miracle in which we are invited to take part. In some sense, we can *be* the miracle.

We tend to devalue small things. Jesus never does. Instead, he points to the power in small things that we might so easily overlook. The largest of all realities—the kingdom of God— housed in the smallest of all seeds, the mustard seed. The pinch of yeast that leavens the whole loaf. A scrap of bread that can

196

help feed a multitude. The miracle can start with what is already in your pocket.

Prayer

God, I seem to have so little to offer, but I know you particularly like to work with small things, so help me to offer it and to leave the rest to you. Amen.

Even with the Best of Intentions

I do not understand my own actions. For I do not
do what I want, but I do the very thing I hate.

—from Romans 7:15–25

Oftentimes we excuse our own actions by focusing on our intentions: "Well, I know this didn't turn out too well, but I had good intentions." For Paul, however, his own good intentions only make his behavior that much harder to take. He is left with this anguishing gap between his intentions and his actions, leading him to rail against himself: "I do not understand my own actions. For I do not do what I want, but I do the very thing I hate."

There is a story of one worshiper who could always be counted on to offer the same prayer week after week: "Lord, sweep the cobwebs from my soul." Each week the same prayer, until finally another worshiper pleaded, "Dear God, kill the spider!" Sometimes we confront the truth that there are no easy fixes for what ails us. Something more drastic is required.

So Paul asks, "Who will rescue me?" Most of us would like to think that we can rescue ourselves with our own best efforts. For the most part, we put our trust in whatever can be added to our to-do list. In this approach, Jesus becomes something like a coach, encouraging us to do our best, teaching us and showing us how it's done. Paul, however, has seen too much and tried too hard to believe that is enough. Our intentions may be consistently good, but our actions . . . well, it's a spotty record at best. Paul knows he needs more than a coach. He needs a Redeemer.

Prayer

I ask with Paul, "Who will rescue me?" But I also offer his prayer of gratitude, "Thanks be to God through Jesus Christ our Lord." Amen.

Addressed by Name

Thus says the Lord . . . Do not fear, for I have redeemed
you; I have called you by name, you are mine.

—Isaiah 43:1

Many people have called me Marty . . . once. I always correct
them: "My friends call me Martin." I don't like being rude, but
I dislike being called Marty even more. But there is more to it.
Quite simply, Marty is not my name. I do not feel addressed by
it. It is someone else's name.

It is almost axiomatic that nothing is as musical to the ear
as the sound of one's own name. That is not from sheer vanity.
Rather, we long to be addressed, for words to find us where
we live. Each of us wants to be recognized as an individual.
We yearn to be known, and known by name. The use of one's
name symbolizes such ties between people and can actually help
create them.

So when scripture says that God calls each one by name,
this comes as a welcome assurance. It implies that God is not
an impersonal force. If God knows me by name, it means that
God is a being and, what is more, a being who seeks to be in
relationship with me. It is one of God's ways of reaching out
to me in all my particularity, as the person I really am. That's
why, when God calls me by name, I am quite sure God uses the
name I feel most addressed by, the name I hear in my dreams.
That is, when God calls me by name, God doesn't say, "Rev.
Copenhaver" or "Marty." Rather, God calls me Martin, because
that's not just my name—it is who I am.

Prayer

O God of many names, I rejoice that you call me by my one
name, the name I hear in my dreams. Amen.

What Can You Give to the God Who Has Everything?

You'll not likely go wrong here if you keep
remembering that our Master said, "You're
far happier giving than getting."
—from Acts 20:32–35

When I was a child, my parents gave me many gifts—not only at Christmas but throughout the year, and not just gifts of toys but gifts of life and love. Indeed, everything I had and everything I am was a gift from their hands.

They did not give me these gifts because I deserved them. And there was nothing I could give in return, even if they were looking to be repaid.

But even as a child, I longed to be the giver of gifts instead of always being the receiver. So one year I wrapped the plaster of Paris handprint paperweight I had made in school and put it under the tree.

I have no reason to believe my parents were eager to receive a handprint paperweight. To be sure, now I can see they did not need it. But when they opened the package, it was with "oohs" and "ahs." They thanked me and embraced me.

They did not need such a gift, but I think they saw I needed to give it. And when my mother died, among the items my siblings and I discovered in her apartment, carefully wrapped in tissue paper and safely placed in a drawer, was that paperweight. The gracious givers of everything I had and everything I am became, for my sake, the gracious receivers of my gift to them.

I think God does the same for us. God needs nothing from us. Indeed, everything we have and everything we are, we have received from God's hand. We cannot give anything in return. What can you give to the God who has everything?

But God also sees that we feel a need to respond, and God allows us to do just that by receiving our gifts of praise and devotion. And the God who has given us everything graciously receives that gift.

Prayer

Thank you, God, for being both a gracious giver and a gracious receiver of gifts. Amen.

Receiving Compliments, Offering Praise

For I will not venture to speak of anything except
what Christ has accomplished through me . . .
by word and deed, by the power of signs and
wonders, by the power of the Holy Spirit.

—from Romans 15:14–21

What do you do when someone pays you a compliment? Do you find yourself standing a little taller because you feel proud of yourself? Or do you try to brush it off by, say, looking down at your feet and muttering something like, "Aw, shucks, it was nothing"?

The apostle Paul probably would take issue with either of those responses. Here, in his letter to the church in Rome, he affirms that anything he has been able to accomplish has been through the power of the Holy Spirit. He is something like the wick that knows it dare not take credit for the flame.

Paul would not presume to take credit for what he has accomplished. And he certainly would not brush it off, either. Instead, it is an occasion for something like awe and reverence.

Imagine: Through the Holy Spirit, the power of the living God is able to work in surprising places, and even in perhaps the most surprising place of all—our own lives. Even through lives like ours.

So when we receive a compliment, a better response than "Thank you" might be "Thank God." Rather than an occasion for either pride or humility, it can be an occasion for praise.

Prayer
God, mine is the wick and yours is the flame, so I praise you, I praise your holy name. Amen.

The God of Second Chances

God, my God, I yelled for help and you put me together. God, you pulled me out of the grave, gave me another chance at life when I was down-and-out.
—Psalm 30:2 MSG

I love officiating at weddings for second marriages. In fact, I often prefer them to weddings for first marriages. I know that might sound strange because, of course, you cannot have a second marriage without the first ending either in death or divorce, two of the saddest realities of all.

But in my experience, people who are getting married a second time approach their weddings differently. They tend not to get taken in by the shimmering surface of weddings. They seem to care less about where they will hold a reception and what the wedding party will wear. They wouldn't want a fairytale wedding, even if they could pull one off. To those who have been married before, all the obsessive focus on the details of a wedding can seem irrelevant, if not downright distracting.

People who are getting married a second time just seem to understand that, in the end, the wedding does not matter all that much. It is the marriage that counts. Perhaps that is why the marriage vows sound different when spoken by someone who has been married before. When someone who could not, or would not, stay in a previous marriage stands up before others and promises to another "for better or for worse," those words take on added resonance. It is clear what is at stake. Or when someone whose first spouse has died utters the words "as long as we both shall live" to another, the vow seems all the more precious. There is no escaping the profound implications of what is going on here.

Besides, I believe in the God of second chances, a God who takes the raw stuff of death or defeat and breathes new life into it.

Prayer

I thank you that you are both the God of new beginnings and the God of second chances. Amen.

God's Amazing and Sneaky Grace

One [of the visitors] said to Abraham, "I will surely
return to you in due season and your wife Sarah shall
have a son." . . . Now Abraham and Sarah were old,
advanced in age; it had ceased to be with Sarah after
the manner of women. So Sarah laughed to herself.

—from Genesis 18:1–15

When a visitor tells Abraham that he and Sarah are about to have a son, Sarah is on the other side of the tent door, listening to the whole conversation. At this announcement, she can't suppress her laughter. After all, she is over ninety years old and Abraham has already hit one hundred, so she laughs, as someone has put it, at the thought of a baby being born in the geriatric ward, with Medicare picking up the tab. She might also be laughing at the holy irony that although she had hoped for a child for so many years, the announcement came after she had given up hope.

God's grace is amazing, but also sneaky. Look to the north and it may come from the south. Look for it eagerly at one particular time and it may arrive just when you have ceased to look for it. Even when we have given up all hope, that does not mean that God has given up acting in our lives.

The key is to be open to God's grace when it sneaks up on us. Under such circumstances it is appropriate to laugh—particularly to laugh at ourselves, that we had looked away just when God was preparing to show up.

Prayer

O gracious and surprising God, I expect so much from you. May I also be open to your movement in my life when you act in unexpected ways and when I have ceased to look for you. Amen.

Escaping Family Legacies

In those days they shall no longer say:
"The parents have eaten sour grapes, and
the children's teeth are set on edge."
—from Jeremiah 31:27–30

In one way or another, we are all wrestling with our family legacies.

A circle of women are having lunch. One says, "I worry every day that I am becoming my mother." Everyone else at the table laughs. Except one. She shakes her head and says, "That's no joke."

A father sits down with his young teenage son and says, "Your uncle just went into rehab. He's an alcoholic. So was your grandfather. That means you've got to be careful, all right? It's got to stop with this generation."

A boy brings home a report card with mostly Ds and a few Cs. When his parents have finished lecturing him, the boy asks, "Well, what do you think it is? Heredity or environment?"

The influence of family legacies may be so strong that it may seem as if we are bound by them—as if bound to something inescapable and inevitable.

Jeremiah is speaking to a people living under foreign rule. He contends that the people must have done something to deserve God's wrath—and if they haven't done something to deserve this, perhaps their parents or grandparents did, and the current generation is paying the price. We might want to argue with his theology, but there it is.

But then Jeremiah envisions a brighter time, when God will redeem God's people. And one aspect of this redemption is that the people will no longer be burdened by their family legacies. He puts it this way: "In those days they will no longer say, 'The parents have eaten sour grapes, and the children's teeth are set on edge.'"

In other words, we may still be sinners. Nevertheless, we will not need to pay for the sins of those who have gone before us.

Our family legacies can seem inescapable, inevitable. Nevertheless, says our God. Nevertheless.

Prayer

God, I thank you for my family legacy, but I also thank you for making it so that I am not bound by that legacy. Amen.

The Separating Power of Possessions

> Their possessions were too great
> for them to dwell together.
> **—from Genesis 36:1–8 ESV**

Jacob and Esau, the twin brothers whose tussles began in their mother's womb, eventually reconciled enough to be able to settle in the same neighborhood in Canaan. They prospered but then became the victims of their own success. The land was not able to support the cattle herds of both brothers, so Esau had to move away. This was a matter of environmental sustainability, but also something more. As the author of Genesis put it, "Their possessions were too great for them to dwell together."

This is not an ancient problem. Today—whether it's in Canaan or New Canaan—prosperity has a way of separating us. In the early 2000s, the fastest-growing segment of the housing market was exclusive gated communities, whose chief attraction is the way they separate people. Even if you don't live in a gated community, if you have enough money to buy sugar in large quantities, you are less likely to have to go next door to borrow a cup from a neighbor. When you have your own car, you never meet your neighbor at the bus stop.

Our prosperity can be too great for us truly to dwell with one another. There is another way of putting it: Sometimes the more wealth we have, the more impoverished our lives can become. Is there a way you can think of to keep your possessions from coming between you and your neighbor?

Prayer

God, everything I have is a gift from you. May I express my thanks by never letting my possessions create distance between me and those around me. Amen.

This Day

This is the day that the Lord has made;
let us rejoice and be glad in it.

—from Psalm 118

As I mentioned before, I am a very future-oriented person. I have a calendar that contains pages for the present year but also for two years ahead. I can tell you now what I am going to preach about months from now. I have a special drawer where I keep tickets to plays or games or trips I look forward to. When that drawer is empty, I get almost panicked.

None of that is bad, I suppose, but being such a future-oriented person sometimes keeps me from appreciating the only day I can live in, and that is today.

Those of us who are farsighted—both literally and figuratively—can see things at a distance but have a hard time seeing what is right under our noses.

That is why when I read this psalm, I try to emphasize the very first word: "This is the day that the Lord has made . . ."

That single word *this* is often the reminder I need. This is the day that God has made and given to me, to all of us, as a gift. This is the day that will have the power to bless, if I let it. This is the day I can make a difference in the world, even if in only one small corner of it, if I choose to. This is the day to enjoy, if I will allow myself to.

Not tomorrow. Or the next year. This day.

Prayer

God, thank you for the gift of this day. Open my heart to receive its blessings and to find in this day ample reason to rejoice. Amen.

Endurance Tests

Love . . . bears all things, believes all things,
hopes all things, endures all things.
—from 1 Corinthians 13:1–8

Early in my ministry, I served First Congregational Church in Burlington, Vermont. Every Wednesday morning for nine years, I led a Bible study with a group made up largely of women in their seventies and eighties. They had been meeting each week for longer than they could remember, which meant, for some of them, since before I was born.

At first, I prepared my lessons with meticulous care, brandishing all the historical-critical methods of scholarship that I had learned in seminary. They would ask follow-up questions, which I took to be something like asking for an encore performance.

Over time, however, the members gently began to redirect the conversation to the ways in which the Bible was speaking to what was going on in their lives. And our time of prayer began to stretch as they lovingly brooded over the congregation with their intercessions.

The first big snowstorm of that winter struck on a Wednesday morning. I couldn't get out of my driveway. Not yet accustomed to life in Vermont, I was surprised that when I called the church office, someone was there to answer the phone. I said, "Quite a storm, isn't it? Obviously, we won't be having Bible study today." The person on the other end of the line replied, "Well, I'll go tell the ladies . . . they'll be so disappointed."

Sure enough, they were all there with Bibles open, waiting dutifully for their new young minister to show up. They never teased me about it directly, but conversation did turn to weather conditions with suspicious frequency after that.

I am reminded that the word *endure* has two meanings: "to last" and "to put up with a lot." Thankfully, that Wednesday morning Bible study endured in both senses of the word.

Prayer

God, may my love of your people endure—truly last—even though that means I will need to put up with a lot. Amen.

Nostalgia Ain't What It Used to Be

No eye has seen, nor ear heard, nor the
human heart conceived, what God has
prepared for those who love him.
—from 1 Corinthians 2:6–13

This morning I picked through musty artifacts in our basement in search of one item, and I was waylaid by many others. There was the spongy ball our son and I used to play epic games of hoops when he was little, a program from our daughter's first dance recital, an article about our wedding from Karen's hometown newspaper, a note my mother sent to me at college, the deed to our first house. I could go on, of course, and I did this morning, wading into all of those items until I was chest deep—heart deep—in nostalgia.

Nostalgia is a very natural and powerful emotion, particularly for those of us who are older. But nostalgia has its dangers. If it gives us renewed appreciation for the ways God has blessed us in the past, then it can be a wonderful occasion for thanksgiving. But nostalgia also can make us idealize the past, and in ways that make the present pale by comparison. So nostalgia can rob the present of delight and the future of hope.

As Christians, we draw on the past in myriad ways, of course, but our faith is always forward-leaning. We are assured that the good old days, no matter how good, are nothing compared to what God has in store for us. Paul quotes Isaiah to remind the Corinthians and perhaps also himself: "No eye has seen, nor ear heard, nor the human heart conceived, what God has prepared for those who love him." So look back, yes. But lean forward.

Prayer
God of yesterday, today, and tomorrow, help me to look back in ways that keep me leaning forward. Amen.

Room to Grow

Dress yourself with the Lord Jesus Christ, and
don't plan to indulge your selfish desires.
—Romans 13:14 CEB

When, as a boy, I went shopping for clothes with my mother, she would always ask me to try on items that were about a size too large to fit me perfectly. If the jeans I tried on were a bit long, she considered them just right, because they left me "room to grow." Until I grew into them, I could fold the pant legs at the bottom—not much of a fashion statement, to be sure, but at least that way I wouldn't need another pair of jeans quite so soon.

Wearing clothes that don't fit perfectly can make you look and feel foolish at times, but it is also a statement to the world that you intend and expect to continue growing. It is not a fashion statement. It is an aspirational statement.

That is how I understand the apostle Paul's admonition to the Romans: "Dress yourself with the Lord Jesus Christ." He is asking the Romans to assume some of the qualities of Christ, to wear them as they would a new set of clothes.

That's quite a charge. When I dress myself with Jesus, I can feel like that boy who is trying to wear an outfit that is at least a size too large. Not only do I feel awkward, but I can even look a bit silly.

Then I remember my mother insisting that it is important to leave "room to grow." What causes me to trip all over myself today allows for the possibility for growth. I put on Jesus as I would a new and ill-fitting outfit—in order that someday it might fit and be a fitting expression of whom I have become.

Prayer

Thank you, Jesus, for leaving me room to grow. Now, please, provide the growth. Amen.

Making Room for the Familiar Stranger

She wrapped him in a blanket and laid him in a manger, because there was no room in the hostel.

—from Luke 2:6–7 MSG

I have always loved the writings of Dylan Thomas. So when our children were still young, I was excited to take my family to a play adapted from Thomas's story called *A Child's Christmas in Wales*. It was a smashing success. Our children were enthralled. I was delighted to think we had created a new family holiday tradition.

For six years running, we went to see the production. It felt like a Christmas liturgy that did not need to be changed from one year to the next. And I always looked forward to it.

Then one year, the theater company did not stage the play. I had to break the news to my family.

After a few understated expressions of sorrow, our daughter tentatively ventured, "You know, Dad, I think it's really okay. To tell you the truth, I never really did like *A Child's Christmas in Wales*."

Our son immediately jumped in: "I'm so glad to hear you say that. I thought I was the only one."

"You never liked it?" I asked.

"Sorry, Dad. Like . . . never."

I turned to my wife. She just shook her head.

It turns out that no one else in my family enjoyed *A Child's Christmas in Wales*. They all found it excruciatingly boring. But for years they had not told me, and they had not told one another either.

In its fullest sense, hospitality is making room for the stranger. And when we make room for a stranger (whether

214

someone we have never met or someone with whom we share a roof), in all his flaws and odd devotions (like to *A Child's Christmas in Wales*), we are making room for Jesus. After all, Jesus told his followers that when we make room for the stranger, we are making room for him.

Prayer

God, help me to make room for the strangers in my life—both those I don't know and those I know so very well. Amen.

Our Daily Ration

Give us this day our daily bread.

—from Matthew 6:9–15

Considering the lofty heights at which the Lord's Prayer begins ("Our Father, who art in heaven"), a bold and direct plea for daily bread just sounds so basic, so material. And we're not supposed to pray for material things, are we? Isn't prayer for bigger things than that?

But Jesus is talking about bread in his prayer. Real bread. The kind of bread that we can take in our fingers. The kind of bread that fills the stomach. The kind of bread that our bodies need to survive.

As someone once said, "We may not live by bread alone, but we don't live very long without it either."

So this prayer is an urgent plea for the food we need. It has elements of the earliest plea in a human life, the cry of an infant for food. Before we were taught to say, "Give us this day our daily bread," no one had to teach us to wail, "Give me my mother's milk—this instant!"

The Christian faith is about life as we live it, and so is this prayer. We spend a lot of our lives thinking about material things, worrying about material things, working for material things. So why would our prayers not reflect those concerns?

But also: "Give us this day our *daily* bread." Just enough for what we need for one day, a daily ration of bread. As we live one day at a time, we are sustained one day at a time.

Prayer
God, following Jesus, we ask for the food we need this day. May we live in that kind of trust day by day. Amen.

Normal Families

> [Rebekah] called her younger son Jacob and said
> to him, "Your brother Esau is consoling himself by
> planning to kill you. . . . Flee at once to my brother
> Laban in Haran, and stay with him a while . . .
> until your brother's anger against you turns away,
> and he forgets what you have done to him."
> —from Genesis 27

In a town called Normal, Illinois, there is a park containing a lovely sculpture that features a husband and wife embracing and looking lovingly into each other's eyes while their young children sit contentedly on their laps. The sculpture is titled "The Normal Family."

The only trouble with that image of family life is that none of us live in a place that could be described as "normal." That may be why that sculpture is regularly vandalized—the vandals are striking out at an idealized image of the family that none of us can live up to. As a mother once told me, "The only thing normal in our family is the knob that says NORMAL on the clothes dryer."

In contrast to that sculpture, the Bible does not hold up an idealized picture of family life. Instead, the Bible depicts families with rival siblings and tension between the generations. There are marriages and betrayals, children who refuse to honor their parents, and parents who hold back blessings from their children. There is love expressed in many of the families of the Bible, but there are also heated arguments and stony silences, slow-boiling resentments and rifts as wide as a canyon.

So when I hear people refer to biblical family values, I wonder: *Are they talking about the rifts and alienation or about the sibling rivalry and bitter resentments?*

The Catholic author Richard Rohr tells a story of Navajo rug weaving. These beautifully handcrafted rugs are perfectly structured, except for a corner on each rug where an obvious flaw can be found. When he asked why flaws were allowed to remain in such otherwise perfect rugs, he was told, "This is where the spirit moves in and out."

Our families, and the families depicted in the Bible, are far from perfect. They are flawed. Yet it is exactly in those flawed places that the Spirit of God can move and where we can catch a glimpse of grace.

Prayer

May your Spirit move in and out of the imperfections. Where there are flaws, let there be grace. Amen.

Seeing God in the Familiar

They said, "Is not this Jesus, the son of Joseph,
whose father and mother we know? How does he
now say, 'I have come down from heaven'?"
—from John 6:41–51 ESV

It is easy for us to grant that God can be at work in something exotic or distant or dim. It can be more difficult to find God in the familiar and everyday. So it is not surprising that those who knew Jesus best were among the most skeptical about any claims that he had a special relationship with God.

When Jesus refers to himself as the "bread of life" who has come from heaven, those who know him protest: "This is Jesus talking? Joseph's son? That can't be. We know his parents!" We can imagine them going on: "I remember when his baby teeth fell out! I remember when he used to play behind our house. I knew him before he learned the books of the Bible. Surely he cannot be God's anointed one." To be sure, these same people might have believed that the Messiah would come and establish God's reign in a way they could not anticipate. But Joseph's son?

It can be difficult to see God at work in the familiar. There is another way to put it: God's miracles are nowhere more difficult to see than when they occur in front of our eyes.

Prayer

God, give me eyes to see you, not just in the exotic or distant or dim, but also in that which is close and familiar. Amen.

Pray Constantly

Rejoice always, pray without ceasing.
—1 Thessalonians 5:16–17

To "pray without ceasing," as the apostle Paul urges, requires more than setting aside time to pray. To pray constantly, prayer has to be something other than an isolated activity. It has to be woven into the fabric of your life.

Jimmy Carter once estimated that he prays a hundred times a day. I imagine that few of those prayers are with eyes closed and that few begin with "Dear God" and end with "Amen." Rather, I imagine that his life and his prayers are so interwoven that he cannot separate the two.

This is what a day of praying without ceasing might look like: You wake up in the morning and, with God, you think about what awaits you in the day ahead. You pre-live the day as a kind of prayer. At the breakfast table, you open up the newspaper—another day of horrific stories of violence and disaster—and, as you read, you simply think, "God, be in that place; be with those people." You get in your car and the traffic is terrible, so you say to God, "The traffic . . ." and you don't need to say any more, because God knows the way that sentence ends is "and the traffic always makes me tense, because I hate to be late." When you arrive at work, there is a message from your mother. She sounds more confused than ever, so before you pick up the phone, you say to yourself, "God, you've got to help me here." And on like that through the day.

Prayer

Dear One, accompany me through my day. Be with me constantly, as I seek to be constantly aware of you. Amen.

Our Papa in Heaven

When we cry, *"Abba!* Father!" it is that very Spirit bearing witness with our spirit that we are children of God, and if children, then heirs, heirs of God and joint heirs with Christ.

—from Romans 8:12–17

Martin Luther mused that Joseph must have been a wonderful father, since Jesus chose to address God as Father. (Luther also said that his relationship with his own father was so difficult that he couldn't address God as Father without shuddering.) But the term Jesus actually used is even more remarkable—*Abba*, which is an intimate term of endearment, more like "Papa" or "Daddy." The word comes from the gurgling sounds that an infant makes before she has learned to talk.

It is the first "word" an infant utters (and it's typical of a father to assume that the word refers to him: "She's talking to me!"). When Jesus addresses God as *Abba*, it reflects the intimacy of his relationship with God, like an infant's close and trusting relationship with a nurturing parent. When Jesus calls God *Abba*, it also makes clear that even before we have the right words—or any words at all—we have enough with which to approach God. Even our wordless gurgles or sighs too deep for words can be enough.

That someone could have such a close relationship with God is remarkable. But the apostle Paul goes on to affirm a still more remarkable truth: Through Jesus, we are invited to have that kind of relationship with God as well. Not only is Jesus the Son of God but, through him, we are God's daughters and sons, and God is our *Abba*, too.

Prayer

Abba, I thank you that, although you are mighty and mysterious, you also seek an intimate relationship with me, like that of a child and a nurturing parent. Amen.

Strangers in the Same Womb

When her time to give birth was at hand, there were twins in her womb. The first came out red, all his body like a hairy mantle; so they named him Esau. Afterward his brother came out, with his hand gripping Esau's heel; so he was named Jacob.

—from Genesis 25:19–27

Esau and Jacob were twins who didn't even wait to be born for their tussles to begin—they wrestled in their mother's womb. And when Esau was born, his brother's hand was clamped on his ankle, as if they had been competing to see who would be born first.

The twins seemed as different as two people could be. Conflict between them finally exploded when Jacob tricked their father into giving him the blessing intended for Esau.

Esau vowed to kill Jacob and probably would have succeeded if Jacob hadn't hightailed it out of there just in time. It took many years, rife with ill feeling and regret, before they finally reconciled.

It is often said that the world would be a better place if we learned to treat one another as brothers and sisters. The obvious problem with that assertion is that our relationships with those closest to us, including family, are often the most difficult of all.

It may not be coincidence that Jesus said both that we should love our neighbors and that we should love our enemies, because often they are the same person. Throughout the biblical story, we are enjoined to welcome the stranger. It is important to remember that sometimes the stranger is the one with whom we share a roof, a bed, or even a womb.

Prayer
O God of open arms, help me to welcome the stranger, including the one who is very close. Amen.

From Messiah to Martin

For a child has been born for us, a son given
to us; authority rests upon his shoulders; and
he is named Wonderful Counselor, Mighty
God, Everlasting Father, Prince of Peace.

—Isaiah 9:6

It was recently reported that after a baby born in eastern Tennessee was given the name Messiah by his mother, a judge ordered the baby's name changed. In explaining her ruling, the judge declared, "The word *Messiah* is a title that has only been earned by one person and that one person is Jesus Christ."

Although we may question the validity of a judge making such a decision, we have to feel relieved for the baby. I can only begin to imagine the kind of teasing a child would have to endure if his name were Messiah. I picture a sarcastic classmate saying, "Well who died and made you savior of the world? Oh, wait a second . . ."

The mother ended up following the judge's orders by renaming her baby Martin—which, I can say from experience, is a considerable come-down. I have only been teased when I looked up the definition of my name: "Of Mars." The name Martin does leave me open to being called "Marty," a nickname I have never liked, but I don't think the nickname for Messiah would be any better—"Messy," perhaps?

Carrying such a huge title would give that child a lot to live up to. But, now that I think of it, that describes all of us. After all, in the name "Christian" we bear the name of Christ. In that way, our own names are forever associated with the title given Jesus. How daunting. How humbling. How wonderful.

Don't tell the judge. "Christian" is a name I don't want to give up.

Prayer

God, you have given us a lot to live up to, so don't leave us now. Amen.

Father, Son . . . and That Other One

[Paul] said to them, "Did you receive the Holy Spirit
when you became believers?" They replied, "No, we
have not even heard that there is a Holy Spirit."

—from Acts 19:1–10

Even though the Holy Spirit is one of the main characters in
the biblical drama, often she can be treated like an actress who
plays only a bit part. If our liturgies reflected our understanding,
we might be baptized in the name of "the Father, the Son,
and the Other One."

The Bible includes many ways to describe the Holy Spirit:
Comforter, Breath, Spirit of Christ. One of my favorite descriptions
does not come from the Bible but seems to sum up much of
what the Bible says about the Holy Spirit: "The God who comes
up through us." It is through the Holy Spirit that the power and
love of God can be at work—even through people like us.

I think all of us have experienced times when we were
able to persevere through circumstances that, by all accounts,
should have destroyed us. And at other times, our stumbling
attempts to speak the truth somehow revealed glimmers of wisdom
deeper than we thought ourselves capable of. At still other
times, we are able to accomplish tasks that would ordinarily
be beyond us, times when, for some reason, we are different—
stronger, surer, more faithful, more capable—and we are at a
loss to explain why.

We speak of these things as we might speak of a mystery. And
they are a mystery, but this mystery has a name: the Holy Spirit.

Prayer

Come, Holy Spirit, come. Come to me today as Holy Power, as
Comforter, as Breath, as the Spirit of Christ. And inspire me to
believe that you can be at work even through me. Amen.

Put My Tears in Your Bottle

You have kept count of my tossings;
put my tears in your bottle.

—from Psalm 56

There is an ancient Jewish proverb: "What soap is for the body, tears are for the soul."

There is some catharsis in shedding tears. But more, the author of this psalm pleads with God, "Put my tears in your bottle." Imagine! God has a bottle for our tears!

It was an ancient Jewish practice for mourners to have a small bottle in which they could collect their tears. The top had a small hole in it that would allow those tears to evaporate over time, and when the bottle was completely dry, the time of grieving was considered over.

So the psalmist asks God, "Put my tears in your bottle." We don't need to keep our sorrow and our tears in the tight little bottle within us where they are usually kept, burning and vengeful, because God has a bottle for our tears.

It must be a bottle as big as the ocean, because in it are the psalmist's tears, a prophet's tears over injustice, Jesus's tears over the death of his friend Lazarus, parents' tears whose children have died in war, widows' tears, toddlers' tears, spurned lovers' tears, your tears, and my tears, mingling with the tears of countless others from countless sorrows.

When we come to God with our grief, God does not pat us on the head and offer a condescending "Now, now . . ." Rather, God receives our tears like an offering and holds them as if in a bottle, honoring our grief and sharing it.

Prayer
God, thank you for honoring my grief enough to hold it and to share it. Amen.

Good-bye

Peace I leave with you; my peace I give to you. Not
as the world gives do I give to you. Let not your
hearts be troubled, neither let them be afraid.

—John 14:27 ESV

One of the reasons parting is so difficult is that, in parting, we confront our limits. We cannot be both here and there. We cannot be with all the people we care about. We cannot grasp what is ahead without in some way letting go of what is past.

So over and over again in scripture we read of people who, in parting, remind one another of the promises of God. And what other way are we to part? In what other way can we? How else can we leave those we care about, unless we entrust them to the care of God?

That is, after all, what the word *good-bye* means: "God be with you." What else can we say in parting that does not simply wither and fall at our feet as soon as it is said?

God be with you, because I can no longer be with you.

God be with you, because, though now we will have limited ways of expressing care for one another, we are still—all of us—in need of care.

God be with you, because if God is with you and with me, somehow we will still be together.

God be with you, because though none of our lives is much more than a collection of fragments—some of them with jagged edges—God promises to make them complete and make us whole, in God's time.

Indeed, there may be no way to part from those we love without either kidding ourselves or being drawn into the shadow of despair—unless we say "Good-bye."

Prayer

God, be with those who are dear to me and hold them close while we are absent one from another. Amen.